Foreword

Performing magic tricks has been a popular pastime among young and old for thousands of years. Historically, magicians have commanded great power and influence because of the magical effects they have created. Today, the most popular magic performers are TV stars who have achieved international fame.

Collins Magic Tricks is a fascinating guide on how to perform over 60 magic tricks which require the minimum of equipment – in many cases just coins, handkerchiefs and so on – without the need for specialist and expensive apparatus. The book starts with the basic skills and equipment you need, and gives advice on how to practise and develop a good performance. Also included is an easy-to-use glossary of important terms used in performing magic tricks.

Each trick is described with step-by-step instructions, complemented by clear, explanatory diagrams. The tricks are arranged by type, in roughly ascending order of difficulty within each chapter.

Created by the Diagram Group, the book is an attractive companion volume to the same team's *Collins Card Tricks* and *Collins Patience Card Games*.

Contents

2. SILK AND HANDKERCHIEF MAGIC

3. STRING AND ROPE MAGIC

4. PAPER MAGIC

5. MIND MAGIC

6. MATHEMATICAL MAGIC

7. MISCELLANEOUS MAGIC

Using this book

The tricks
Each trick is described as follows:
Effect – what the audience will see happen.
Equipment – all the materials you need to do the trick (it is assumed that a table or flat surface is available).
Preparation – techniques you need to practise and any prop preparation required.
Performing – a step-by-step procedure (with illustrations) explaining how the trick is done.

Skill level
The tricks in this book are arranged into chapters according to the type of props used in the trick. Within each chapter tricks are grouped, more or less, by type, and are arranged roughly in order of increasing difficulty. Each trick is given a difficulty grading of Easy (●), Moderate (◆) or Difficult (✖).
Some tricks are more suitable for older performers because of the skills required. Younger performers may require adult supervision with props such as matches, scissors, knives and glue. These are marked ✚. Most, however, are appropriate for all age levels.

Introduction

A SHORT HISTORY OF MAGIC

According to Arthur Conan Doyle's famous detective
Sherlock Holmes, 'We see but we do not observe.' In
many ways this describes the reaction a magic
performer is trying to instil in his (or her) audience. The
performer wants the spectator to see what is happening,
but not observe what is going on behind the scenes.
Magic tricks have been practised since ancient times.
Probably the earliest record is found in an Egyptian
papyrus dating from 1700 BC. It shows an illusionist,
Dedi of Dedsnefu, performing a trick in front of the
Pharaoh.
The ancient Greeks and Romans had a fondness for
tricks, particularly those using hidden mechanical
devices which produced miraculous effects. Using such
devices, priests could make temple doors open
automatically and wine flow from the mouths and arms
of statues. The Cups and Balls trick (see p. 241) was
described by a Roman named Seneca in the 1st century
BC. It is still commonly performed today.
In medieval Europe, the practice of magic became
associated with witchcraft, a practice which was
punishable by death. Nevertheless, some performers
used their abilities to exert power and influence over
God-fearing people.
In 1584, the Englishman Reginald Scot, in his book *The
Discoverie of Witchcraft*, tried to show how magic
tricks were performed – by sleights of hand, not the
work of the devil. His text explained the secrets of

many magic tricks, including those using coins, cards and ropes. He wrote the book to expose the work of magicians, but instead it became the first manual for practising magicians.

Even by the late 16th century, performing magic tricks was not considered respectable. Nevertheless, novelty acts such as fire- and sword-swallowing, and performances using 'intelligent' animals, were popular in fairs and markets.

In 18th-century Britain, performers of magic tricks had gained some respectability, and perhaps the most famous was Isaac Fawkes. He amassed a fortune from performing close-up tricks at fairs and at private parties in the homes of wealthier citizens.

The late 18th and early 19th centuries saw the appearance of several hundred professional magicians. By the early 19th century 'scientific' tricks were in vogue and performers calling themselves Doctor or Professor wove inventive stories to explain their tricks in terms of 'science'. For example, the French magician Jean Eugène Robert-Houdin explained his famous levitation trick (raising a person in the air without any apparent support) in terms of the newly-discovered gas, ether. His explanation was false, but it was a convincing part of his performance. Robert-Houdin was to become a legendary figure among magicians and was later dubbed 'The Father of Modern Magic'. Originally a watchmaker and inventor, he did not become a full-time magician until over 50 years old. He made many improvements to the techniques and equipment then fashionable. He developed his magic craft to a very high standard and was instrumental in bringing greater respect to the profession.

The late 19th century and early 20th century was the great age of travelling shows. Spectacular magic shows travelled from theatre to theatre, in Europe and the United States. Such was the popularity of magic shows that one magician and entrepreneur, John Nevil Maskelyne, was able to run a permanent magic theatre in London for over 40 years from 1873.

As magic shows became more popular, and there was greater competition between performers, speciality acts arose and performers developed special personas (theatrical characters). One of the most famous was William Ellsworth Robinson, a white American, who wore makeup and performed as the Chinese magician Chung Ling Soo, even inventing a 'mock-Chinese' language. He took the performance far beyond the stage, and kept up his Chinese persona at all times in public. He died on stage in 1918, attempting his famous trick in which he caught a bullet in his mouth. The gun was faulty and fired a real bullet that killed him.

Perhaps the most famous magic performer of all time was Harry Houdini, who was born in 1874 in Budapest, Hungary, as Ehrich Weiss. During his career as an escapologist he challenged several police forces to lock and bind him in chains and sacking. On each occasion he was able to free himself, sometimes in very unusual circumstances (on one occasion he was lowered into New York harbour in a safe, and escaped). He died in performance on 31 October 1926, Hallowe'en. Several days beforehand he had challenged some students to

Chung Ling Soo

punch him in the stomach, saying that he could withstand any blow. One student punched him before he had time to tense his stomach muscles. This blow ruptured his appendix and was the cause of his death several days later.

One of the more interesting 20th-century performers was Cardini, who learnt his card-handling skills in the long days spent as a soldier in the trenches during World War I. He wore gloves to keep out the cold. Later, as a performing conjuror, white gloves and a monocle were his trademark, and on stage he would produce dozens of fans of cards from nowhere. His performance also included pretending to be drunk while producing a succession of bizarre articles while handing his clothes to a valet.

The demise of variety and vaudeville shows in the 1950s reduced the opportunities for performing magic on stage. However, the best magicians who specialized in close-up magic or stage magic for cabaret or television continued to make a living, and many travelled internationally. There are still many opportunities for performing magic in small venues such as social clubs, and in larger venues such as theatres and nightclubs, and, through the medium of television, performers can reach a worldwide audience.

TYPES OF MAGIC PERFORMANCE

Children's magic

Many magicians make a full- or part-time living by
presenting magic shows to children. The performance
usually lasts the best part of an hour. The conjuror
dresses in bright clothes, uses colourful equipment, and
gets the children to join in with performing the tricks.

Close-up magic

Close-up magic is done before a small audience, at
home or in a venue such as a restaurant, although a
performance can be shown on television to a large
audience. The performer uses small items such as cards,
coins and rope. In a restaurant, the conjuror may move
from table to table, performing an act which lasts just
5–10 minutes.

Stand-up magic

A general term for the larger-scale forms of magic
which are performed on stage or for television. Large
props are used and the visual spectacle forms an
important part of the act. Often an assistant is involved.
Performances of the types of magic described below
often fall into this category. The well-known British
magician, Paul Daniels, performs both close-up and
stand-up magic on television.

Escapology

This form of magic involves performers escaping from
devices into which they are locked or bound. The
performer needs to be strong and supple. Escape
usually involves the performer untying knots and
picking locks while in a very constrained position.
Harry Houdini was the most famous exponent of this
form of magic.

Illusions

Illusions are seemingly impossible feats performed with large objects, often people; for example, making a person disappear or sawing a person in half. Performing illusions usually requires large and expensive equipment plus the help of one or more assistants. The American David Copperfield and the double-act Siegfried and Roy are famous illusionists.

Mentalism (mind-reading)

These tricks give the appearance of being performed by superhuman feats of the mind. They vary from predicting the future and mind-reading (clairvoyance) to bending metal forks and stopping watches. Al Koran, Kreskin and Uri Geller are famous exponents of mentalism.

Silent magic

A performance without any speech. The performer's gestures and expressions are used to convey meaning. This is a very challenging form of magic, since the visual aspect is so important and speech cannot be used to misdirect attention. Success depends on costume, visual props and the effective use of mime.

Harry Houdini

WHAT YOU WILL NEED

Before you start on the road to becoming a magician, you need a few things – a surprisingly few things: some everyday items (coins and a handkerchief will do for starters), this book, and patience and enthusiasm. The rest will follow. If you want to plunge straight in and learn a trick, turn to p. 34. If you want some background – and you will need this later anyway – read on.

Props

Props – the theatrical term short for 'properties' – refers to the equipment and other items used by the performer. Props vary from everyday items, such as handkerchiefs and elastic bands, to specially bought or made equipment. You may use a prop simply to demonstrate your conjuring prowess; by making the object disappear, for example. Or the prop itself may make the magic work, such as a wand which can extend and retract or which is hollow. Props are also useful for distracting the audience's attention from secret moves, such as using a magic wand to direct the audience's gaze. Some props, though seeming to be everyday objects, are specially made for the job. For example, wands, silk scarfs and soft rope are best bought from a magic shop, but you can start by using ordinary handkerchiefs and ropes.

The clothes you wear can be props in themselves: a silk scarf tied about the head, concealed pockets in a jacket, or a belt or sash around the waist concealing items. A top hat or pointed hat and wand are traditional props which are strongly associated with magic. Seeing them instantly tells people you are a magician.

Here are some dos and don'ts when using props.

Dos

● Mix special magic props with everyday objects. People are often more amazed by magic done with everyday items than with made-for-the-purpose props.

● Be imaginative and use objects different from the norm. Use an apple or orange, for example, instead of a ball.

● Match the props to your audience. Brightly coloured props work well with a young audience. A mind-reading act with an adult audience will require more subdued colours.

● Think about how your props will appear to the audience. Are they attractively set out? Will they be visible? (Red props will not show up against red clothing.) Will the colours clash?

● Keep your props clean and in good order. They are all part of your image and they need to look good and work well.

● If you can, choose a theme – say, an Oriental or Egyptian one – and make sure your props follow this theme.

● Think carefully about your clothes. If necessary, make sure they have suitably placed pockets (secret or otherwise) for holding your props.

● Make a suitably coloured magic box – decorated with magic signs – to keep your smaller props in.

Don'ts

● Don't use too many props. If you can use the same prop in several tricks, do so.

● Don't leave your props lying around so a spectator can inspect them.

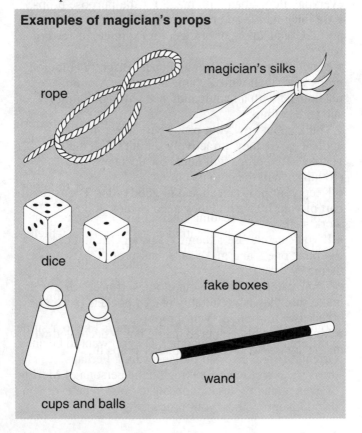

Examples of magician's props

rope

magician's silks

dice

fake boxes

cups and balls

wand

A persona

Your persona is the character or image you project as a performer. As a conjuror, you want to be liked and you want to be remembered. How can you achieve that? What you say and do, and how you appear to the audience, all build up to give the audience a picture of who you are. Think carefully about this. What impression do you want to create? How do you want your audiences to remember you? What kind of audiences do you want to play to anyway?

When you have decided what your character (your persona) will be, this will make your choice of costume, props and the tricks themselves much clearer. You will be on your way to developing your own style. Do you want to be funny or simply friendly and casual? Do you want to concentrate on close-up tricks? Or do you want to perform on a stage doing tricks with larger props? Do you want to do both? Do you want to incorporate mind-reading (mentalism) in your act? In this book we have concentrated on those tricks which need the minimum of equipment and do not require large props. This is, in any case, your most likely starting point as a performer. Later, you may wish to perform as an illusionist using larger props on a big stage.

Consider what to wear. Some performers like to assume a different character altogether. Do you want to be an Oriental magician or an Indian swami? Perhaps dressing as a clown, or taking on the persona of Merlin or even a mad professor appeals to you? Whatever you decide, your clothes, your props and your entire

presentation – what you say and do – need to be
convincing. They all need to work together to create an
overall impression. So, if you have chosen to be Merlin,
make sure that your props reflect this, and are painted
with suitable symbols and in appropriate colours.
Whatever you decide, make sure you are comfortable
as this character. If not, be yourself.

Patter
Your patter is what you say and how you say it – during
your performance. This will depend, among other
things, on the persona you have adopted, the nature of
your audience, and how confident you feel. Most of us
are somewhere between being shy and being very
confident. Performing itself increases self-confidence,
and some people who are otherwise quite shy find they
blossom on stage and have no trouble in commanding
the attention of an audience. In many cases, a casual
and friendly style of presentation works well. Use
humour if you are comfortable doing so and it fits in
well with your persona, and is geared to your audience.

Here are some dos and don'ts regarding patter.

Dos
● Plan carefully what you are going to say, from start to
finish. It helps to write this down in note form,
indicating each point you want to make.
● Practise your presentation in a room on your own
with a tape recorder. Stand up and deliver your
performance as though an audience is there. Play back
the tape and you will probably discover that there are
many mistakes, pauses, repetitions and so on. Don't

worry. Keep practising, and taping, and you will discover that your performance will soon improve.

● Once you have developed some confidence, practise your patter in front of those you know and trust. Ask them for their comments.

● Do respond to the audience. As your confidence develops you will find that you talk with greater and greater ease.

● Invent stories to explain and enhance your tricks.

● Use patter to misdirect the audience from what you are doing.

● Speak clearly and slowly.

● Make sure you speak loudly enough so that the person at the back can hear.

● If you are going to use a microphone, practise using it before a performance. On the day, check that the microphone is properly set up and then leave it alone. Wherever possible, use a clip-on microphone rather than a microphone on a stand, so that you are not restricted from moving around.

Don'ts

● Don't talk too much. Avoid a running commentary.

● Don't state the obvious, such as 'Here is a yellow box.'

● Don't insult anyone.

● Don't drop your voice at the end of a sentence. If anything, raise it.

Working with an assistant

Working with an assistant does have several
advantages.

● Instead of having to work with all the props in place
beforehand, each trick can be brought in as it is needed.

● The assistant can distract the audience's attention
while you, the performer, complete a move.

● The assistant may even perform the trick move him-
or herself.

● Having an assistant increases the range of tricks you
can do and the banter between you and your assistant
creates greater interest for the audience and helps fill
out the act.

● Your assistant can also help you develop and improve
your tricks.

But having an assistant means that there is, so to speak,
an extra mouth to feed. If you are performing for
money, the money will need to be split. Many conjurors
and magicians cannot, or choose not to, have an
assistant.

Working with an assistant is very different from
working with a confederate (or stooge). This is a person
who pretends to be an ordinary member of the audience
but who secretly helps the performer accomplish the
trick. Using a stooge is frowned upon by most
magicians – they consider it a form of cheating.

PREPARATION

Simply knowing how a trick is done and how to carry it out will not make you a successful performer. You are still only halfway there. You need to entertain the audience and convince them – by all your actions – that something exciting is happening. This takes practice – and lots of it.

Here are the dos and don'ts of preparation for mastering a trick.

Dos

● Learn one trick at a time.

● Learn the trick thoroughly so that you are absolutely confident how to present it.

● Learn a few tricks well, rather than many tricks sloppily.

● Imagine what the trick will be like from the audience's point of view. Will it be interesting? Will they spot something they aren't meant to see? How can you distract them so they won't notice what you're doing with the props? How can you finish the trick in a dramatic way?

● Continue working on a trick, and making adjustments, until you are completely happy with it. This may mean the trick is slightly different from the way it is described here – but you will have made the trick your own.

● Adjust your finger positions if you find a particular move difficult or awkward – not everyone's hands are the same.

● Track down the weak spots in a trick and work out ways to get around them, using misdirections if necessary.

● Practise frequently but in small doses. You are more likely to overcome a problem when you come to it afresh.

● Practise in front of a mirror. It helps 'fine-tune' your performance and allows you to see how it looks from the audience's point of view. It also encourages you to look away from your hands and at the audience.

● Try a new trick on friends and family, and listen to their comments.

● Make the props yourself or buy them from a reputable dealer in magic equipment. You can then be sure you are using reliable equipment which looks good, does the job and will last.

● Remember, first and foremost, you are an entertainer – you must make your performance lively, interesting and enjoyable.

Don'ts

● Don't show any trick until you have practised it thoroughly.

● Don't perform a trick until you can do it so well that you don't have to worry about 'what comes next'.

● Don't tense up at the crucial point in a trick. Practise until you make the difficult move look casual and easy.

● Don't tell anyone how the trick is done.

There is a saying among magic-trick performers: 'Practise. Practise again. Practise until you can do it perfectly. Then practise some more.'

PERFORMING

A performance of magic – whether a single trick or a whole routine – is not merely a collection of bits cobbled together. You need to prepare your performance as a whole piece, with a start and a finish. Think through your act carefully so that it is smooth and polished. One trick or part of the act should follow on naturally from another.

The structure of a performance

When you plan your performance you need to take into account the kind of audience and the venue. Is it a small venue where you can perform close-up magic, or is it a larger one, where you will be performing on stage? A performance of close-up magic for an adult audience would typically last 10–15 minutes and use six to eight tricks. A performance on stage would normally last slightly longer. If you were performing at a children's party, you would probably use fewer tricks, but make each trick last much longer and involve the children more. You might weave a story around each trick. Here are some suggestions as to what you might include, whatever the type of performance:

● At the beginning do quick and easy tricks which allow you to relax and let the audience get to know you. Simple production or vanishing tricks are suitable here.

● In the middle of the performance, when you and the audience are more relaxed, use longer, more complicated tricks which involve the spectators more. Tricks with long story lines or those involving mentalism (mind-reading) are suitable here.

● Build up to the end of your performance with a couple of straightforward tricks, and then try to finish on a spectacular visual trick. The production of a large number of items – the more silks, or whatever, the better – or the reappearance of an object you made vanish earlier in your performance – are good tricks with which to finish your act.

Here are the dos and don'ts in preparing for and during the performance.

Dos – Preparing the performance

● Choose tricks which are suitable for the kind of audience you are expecting.

● Read about magic and magicians, and use every opportunity you can to look at magicians as they perform. Analyse what they do and learn from it.

● Plan your performance in detail.

● Think about having music playing in the background when you first enter the room to perform. This music should fit in with your persona, the type of performance and your audience.

● Decide in which order you are going to do the tricks, and how one trick will lead on to the next.

● Inject variety into your act. To the performer, the tricks work in different ways. To the spectator, the tricks may appear similar. Make sure you emphasize the differences between tricks and include a variety of tricks that involve more than one person, where objects are revealed in different ways, and where various props are used.

● Work out what to say from start to finish.

● Vary the pace of your performance; for example, intersperse slow tricks with fast ones.

● Be aware of your own strengths and weaknesses and tailor your performance to make the most of your strengths.

● Make sure your hands and fingernails are clean and that you are neat and well groomed. Even if you are wearing casual clothes, make sure you look clean and tidy.

● Make sure you have all your props in the right places at the start of the performance. Decide carefully what you wish the audience to see.

● Expect to get excited and anxious before a performance. Professionals do.

● Practise regularly and pay attention to detail. This increases confidence in your performance and reduces the chances of getting stage fright – an attack of nerves on stage.

● Run through everything in your routine and check that everything is where it should be – and works.

● Make sure that you have an alternative plan – a trick held in reserve – should something unexpectedly go wrong or because, for whatever reason, you have to abandon a trick.

● Take a dozen deep breaths before walking on stage. It calms your nerves and allows you to concentrate on entertaining your audience.

Dos – During the performance
● Walk confidently to the spot where you are going to perform.

- Beam a smile at your audience and move your eyes around the room to try and make everyone feel as though you have noticed them – as individuals.
- Choose a trick you can do well as your first number.
- Speak clearly and slowly.
- Tell a story, make a joke – above all, entertain – but do it naturally. Be yourself. Find your own style.
- Be prepared to make changes during your performance if things go wrong.
- Use your hands and eyes to direct the audience where you want them to look.
- Use explanations and patter to misdirect the audience from what you are actually doing.
- Ask a spectator to show a chosen item to someone else. This prevents the possible embarrassment of the spectator later forgetting the item, or even purposely naming another item to spoil the trick.
- Act relaxed and smile. Look as though you are enjoying yourself.
- React to your own tricks. Scratch your head, shrug your shoulders, and so on to help convey your feelings.
- Use the rhythm of your speech to create drama. Talk slowly to show concentration and build suspense. Talk louder and faster at the climax of a trick.
- At appropriate points in your performance when you can expect some applause, take a small bow or open your palms towards the audience and pause, looking at them. Such actions usually trigger applause.
- Think about your performance and constantly strive to improve your presentation.
- Aim to make the audience believe – by your words,

movements and appearance – that you are truly a
successful magician.
● Leave the audience wanting more.
● At the end of the performance, thank your audience
and take a bow. Leave before the applause finishes.

Don'ts – During the performance
● Don't do two similar tricks in the same performance.
● Don't repeat a trick (unless the trick is specifically
designed to be repeated).
● Don't try to do a trick if you are not confident about
it – you are likely to give a poor performance.
● Don't speak too fast. This is easy to do if you are
nervous. Slow down.
● Don't spoil a surprise by stating what will happen
before it does.
● Don't turn your back on the audience if you can avoid
it. To move backwards, step back or move diagonally
across.
● Don't insult anyone – whether they are present or not.
● Don't take everything so seriously that if things go
wrong your act falls apart. Laugh with everyone else
and then get on with the next trick.

GLOSSARY

The following is a list of some of the terms you will
need to know when performing tricks or talking to
other magicians. It would be particularly useful to
memorize them and to practise the various palming
sleights.

backpalm A sleight that allows the hand to be shown
empty while concealing something behind the fingers
(**a**).
bight A loop of rope, string or similar contained in a
knot.
changing bag A bag with two (or more) compartments,
used for exchanging one item for another.
close-up magic Tricks designed to be performed close
to the audience.
false count A count of items which appears genuine
but where the number of items is actually more or less
than it seems to be.
finale The finish to a trick or an act – usually the high
point of the performance.

fingerpalm Concealing an item between the fingers of a hand (**b**).

force To give a spectator an apparently free choice but really making him or her select an object of the performer's choice.

gimmick A secret piece of equipment (sometimes called a **fake**).

glimpse To view an item secretly.

homing The magical return of an object to its original place after it has seemingly disappeared.

lapping The art of secretly dropping items on the lap while seated at a table.

mentalism Using physical methods to give the appearance of mind-reading or clairvoyance.

misdirection The art of drawing the spectator's attention away from a secret move.

move The execution of a SLEIGHT or other secret manoeuvre.

one ahead A principle of MENTALISM in which the performer is at least one move ahead of the audience.

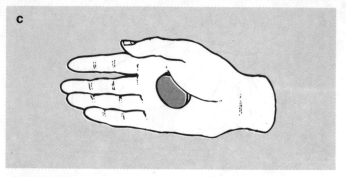

palming Concealing an item in the palm of the hand (**c**).

patter The speech – story line, jokes and so on – used by a performer during an act.

production Making objects appear from thin air or from an apparently empty container.

props Objects used by a conjuror in performing a trick.

pull A GIMMICK, often worked by elastic, that makes an item vanish by pulling it up the sleeve or beneath a jacket.

routine The order of events that make up a trick or a series of tricks in a performance.

servante A hidden shelf or suspended pocket, behind a table or chair or otherwise concealed, to receive items discarded or exchanged.

set up The way props are arranged for a trick.

sleight A skilful movement of the fingers by which a trick effect is accomplished.

sleight of hand The performing of SLEIGHTS.

steal To remove something secretly from the place where it is concealed.

stooge Also called a **confederate**. Someone from the audience posing as a volunteer, but who is actually working with the performer to make the trick work.

sucker trick A trick in which the performer lets the audience believe that they have worked out how the trick is done or that they have seen a mistake. The performer then proves them wrong.

switch To exchange one item for another secretly.

talk The accidental sound made by something hidden, thus revealing its presence to the audience.

thumbpalm Concealing an item by holding it at the base of the thumb and first finger (**d**).

wand Originally used to describe the stick claimed to be the source of a magician's power. A wand in one hand is a practical device which can, for example, be used to conceal a small object in the palm or, by pointing, to direct (or MISDIRECT) attention.

1. Coin magic

Magic tricks using coins are popular not only because of people's inherent interest in money, but because coins are small props, immediately to hand, and can be supplied by spectators. In tricks where the performer makes a spectator's coins disappear, the audience feels more involved because someone's money is at stake. Most tricks require medium- to large-sized coins; ten pence pieces, fifty pence pieces or pound coins are particularly useful because they have milled or angled edges which make them easier to handle. Some tricks, such as The Travelling Coin (see opposite), Two Heads Are Better Than One (see p. 37) and Behind The Ear (see p. 48) require no props other than the coins themselves and so can be done anytime and anywhere. Other tricks such as The Dissolving Coin (see p. 58) and Coin In The Wool (see p. 66) are more sophisticated and use several props. Such tricks can provide a dramatic finale to a magic routine.

● THE TRAVELLING COIN

A quick and easy trick which is very convincing if you get the timing right.

Effect

The performer makes a coin magically move from one hand to join a coin in the other hand.

Equipment

Two similar medium- to large-sized coins.

Preparation

The trick depends on the precise positioning of the coins in the hand, and the speed and smoothness with which the hands are turned over. Practise talking as you turn over your hands to help misdirect the audience's attention.

Performing

● Ask members of the audience for two coins of the same type (make sure that you have practised the trick using coins of this type).

● Now show the coins to the audience, one on the palm of each hand. The coins need to be positioned carefully (**1**). The coin in the left hand should be placed between

1

30 cm

the third and fourth fingers. The one on the right should be near the base of the thumb.

● Hold the hands, palms up, about 30 cm (12 in) apart on a table top.

● Explain to the audience that you can make any coin travel through the air at the speed of light.

● At precisely the same moment, turn both hands over so that the thumbs come close together and then draw the hands immediately apart. Your audience will believe that there is one coin beneath each hand. In fact, because of the original positioning of the coins, the coin from the right hand has been thrown under the left (**2**).

● Lift the right hand to show that the coin from that hand has gone.

● Now lift your left hand and show – to your surprised audience – that both coins are there.

◆ TWO HEADS ARE BETTER THAN ONE

This trick is particularly suitable for a young audience.

Effect

In this trick, of moderate difficulty, a spectator's coin appears to have a head on both sides.

Equipment

A medium-sized coin such as a ten pence piece.

Preparation

The trick calls for the precise timing of rapid hand movements which must be practised.

Performing

● Borrow an ordinary ten pence piece from a member of the audience.

● Place the coin on the palm of your right hand, with the head side up. Raise the right hand so that it is slightly above and to the right of your left hand (**1**). Show the coin to your audience.

● Now do the following move to give the appearance that you are turning over the coin. It is described here one step at a time. In reality, you will do the move swiftly and smoothly in a fraction of a second.

● Move your right hand sharply to the right, and move your left hand slightly to the right, so that the coin slides off and drops on to your left hand, still head side up (**2**).

● As the coin falls onto your left hand, turn your right hand over and slap it down on your left hand (**3**). Doing this quickly gives the appearance that the right hand has turned the coin over.

● Now remove your right hand and show the audience that the 'other' side of the coin is also a head (**4**).
● You can repeat the move using both hands. For example, with the coin in your left hand slightly higher than the right, you can pass the coin to your right and appear to make the coin turn over when in reality it hasn't. By passing from right hand to left, and then from left hand to right, it will appear that the coin genuinely has two heads.
● At the end, pick up the coin between the finger and thumb of your right hand and show the audience that it is a genuine two-sided coin. Then return it to the person you borrowed it from.

● NINE TAILS

A simple mathematical puzzle.

Effect

A circle of ten coins is laid head side up. By following a set of rules, a member of the audience tries to turn the coins so nine are tail side up. He fails every time, but the magician can do it in seconds.

Equipment

Ten coins of the same type, and which have a clear head and tail side.

Preparation

Pay particular attention to the patter you will use when demonstrating how the puzzle works.

Performing

● Lay out ten coins head side up in a circle so the edges of each coin are not touching (**1**). Say to the audience that the object of the exercise is to turn nine coins tail side up.

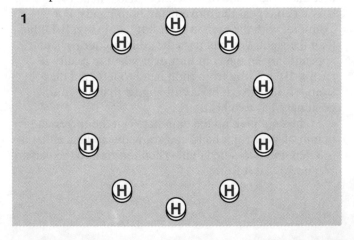

● Explain that there are rules. For each move the player must start on a head, finish on a head and count four places. Each move thus involves starting on a head, counting four coins in a clockwise or anticlockwise direction, and then turning over the fourth coin (which initially is a head but is then turned over tail side up).

● For each move, the player can start anywhere in the circle, providing it is a head.

● Now demonstrate what you have just said (in doing so you will actually demonstrate how the problem is solved, but you will discover that onlookers will not be able to repeat what you have done).

● Reinforce the rules as you go along, but don't explain why you have chosen to start each move from a specific coin.

● Starting anywhere, count one, two, three and turn the fourth coin tail up (**2**). Stop and have a few words with your spectators.

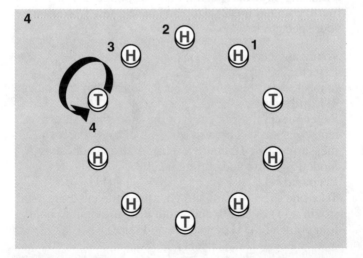

● For the second move, start your count so that it will finish on the coin that you started your first count on (**3**). Stop and chat before the next move.

● For the third move, start so that you finish on the coin you started your second count on (**4**).

● Continue in this way, and you will finish with nine coins tail side up, and one face up.

● Now turn over all the coins so they are face up and ask a member of the audience to follow the rules and finish with nine coins tail side up. He is very unlikely to succeed!

Note: If the audience ask you to show them again how it is done, start in a different place on the circle, and move in a different direction from that of your original demonstration. Don't repeat the demonstration more than once.

● EXTRA MONEY

This straightforward trick is particularly suitable for a young audience.

Effect

In this trick, three coins are joined magically by four others.

✛ Equipment

Seven medium-sized coins of the same type, such as a ten pence piece. Three sheets of thick card, each measuring 20 x 12 cm (8 x 5 in). A strong adhesive. A modelling knife and cutting board.

Preparation

Take one sheet of card and with the knife cut a diagonal slot in it (**1**) of length and width just sufficient to hold four coins of the type you intend to use.

Glue the two other pieces of card, one to each side of the first card so that the cards form a flat tray with a hidden cavity (**2**). Put four coins in this cavity and you are ready to perform the trick.

Performing

● Holding the tray by the corner to conceal the cavity, take three coins and count them out one by one onto the top of the card tray.

● Now show the audience that first your right hand and then your left hand are both empty. As you do this you will need to transfer the tray from left to right hand and then back again. When you do this, make sure that you do not let the audience see the opening to the concealed cavity.

● Now tip the tray so that the coins (including the four in the concealed cavity) slide into the palm of your left hand (**3**).

● At this point the audience expects you to have only three coins in your left hand. Put the tray to one side and open your hand to reveal that it actually holds seven coins. Then take a bow.

● THE HANKIE VANISH

A fairly easy coin vanish involving a member of the audience.

Effect

The performer makes a coin disappear from a handkerchief while a spectator is holding it.

Equipment

A small coin and a large silk handkerchief with a similar second coin sewn into the hem.

Preparation

Prepare a large silk handkerchief by opening the hem at one corner, inserting a small coin, and then sewing the hem up again, making sure the coin is held securely in place (**1**).

1

Performing

● Take the coin in your right hand and hold it up to the audience between finger and thumb.

● With your left hand holding the coin corner of the handkerchief, drape the handkerchief over the coin. In one smooth movement take the coin corner up underneath into the centre of the hankie and thumbpalm the real coin in your right hand (**2**).

2

● Keeping the palmed coin carefully concealed, remove your right hand from under the handkerchief.
● Now get a member of the audience to hold the sewn-in coin through the hankie (**3**).

3

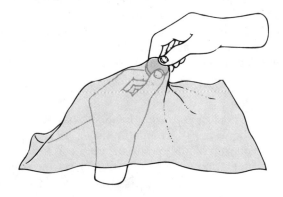

• Now grab hold of a corner of the hankie in your left hand and whisk the hankie away. The coin has vanished!

• Show both sides of the hankie to the audience and then put the hankie away, pocket the palmed coin and get on with the next trick.

◆ BEHIND THE EAR
This trick is of moderate difficulty and is particularly suitable for a young audience.
Effect
The coin disappears from the performer's hand and reappears from behind a spectator's ear.
Equipment
A medium-sized coin such as a ten pence piece.
Preparation
The trick depends on the timing and smoothness of hand movements and needs plenty of practice.
Performing
• Ask a member of the audience for a coin (make sure it is a type of coin you have practised with).

• Hold the coin in your left hand between thumb and fingers and face the audience (**1**).

• Bring your left hand up and bring your right hand

across as if to take the coin. Put your right thumb
behind the coin and your fingers in front (**2**) so
shielding the move from the audience.

● With barely any movement, open the thumb and
fingers of your left hand slightly, letting the coin fall
into the palm of your left hand (**3**). This move is called
the French Drop.

● A split second later, press your right thumb and fingers together as if holding the coin and move them to your right, looking at your right hand as you do so. Your eyes should misdirect the audience into believing that the coin is now in your right hand.

● Casually drop your left hand down by your side, gently gripping the coin with the joints of your fingers.

● Blow on your right hand and open it slowly, showing that the coin has disappeared.

● Now with your left hand reach up behind the ear of the person who gave you the coin. As you do this, push the coin up to your fingertips and let it make contact with the person's ear as you pull your hand away from his head.

● Show the coin in your left hand as you did at the beginning of the trick. Hey presto!

◆ COIN IN THE BUN
A rather unusual vanishing coin trick.
Effect
The performer makes a coin disappear and then reappear from inside a bun.
Equipment
A medium- to large-sized coin and a slightly stale bun or roll.
Preparation
Practise in front of a mirror using some slightly stale buns or rolls to get the technique just right.
Performing
● Use the French Drop technique as described in Behind The Ear (see p. 48). Instead of making the coin

appear from behind the ear of a spectator, make it
appear from inside a bun.

● After showing the audience your empty right hand,
pick up the bun with your left hand (this hand contains
the palmed coin).

● Explain that you have a hunch that the missing coin is
in the bun.

● Start to break open the bun by first bending the sides
up so that the underside of the bun breaks open (**1**).

● With the fingers of your left hand, surreptitiously slip
the coin into the break in the bun (**2**).

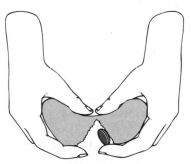

● Now bend the sides of the bun down keeping the lower broken halves together, and the coin will pop up from the middle of the bun (**3**).

3

◆ THE MAGIC WAND

A straightforward vanishing coin trick suitable for performing near the beginning of a magic routine. Make up your own patter and gags to make this trick truly your own.

Effect

The performer transfers a coin from the right hand to the left apparently to make way for another object. In doing so the coin disappears.

Equipment

A medium- to large-sized coin and a wand or pencil.

Preparation

The trick depends on the French Drop sleight of hand (see Behind The Ear, p. 48) but using the right hand instead of the left. This sleight, together with the misdirection needed to divert the audience's interest, needs to be thoroughly practised.

Performing

● Place the coin and wand (or pencil) on a table.
● Pick up the coin with your right hand and show it to the audience, holding the coin by its edges between thumb and first finger (**1**).

● Look at the wand (or pencil) as if you want to pick it up but cannot because the coin is in your right hand. This creates a reason for doing the next step.
● Keep looking at the wand (or pencil) and put your left hand over your right as if to transfer the coin to your left hand. In reality, drop the coin into the fingers of your right hand (**2**, see over). Your left hand hides what is really happening while your eyes direct the audience's attention to the wand.

2

● Now pick up the wand with your right hand, still keeping the coin concealed by holding it in your palm or in the crease of your fingers.

● Turn to look at your left fist, where the coin is meant to be. Tap the left fist with the wand, as if working magic.

● Uncurl your left hand slowly, watching with interest. React with surprise or delight that the coin has gone. Turn and face the audience with your left hand open. This should elicit appreciative applause.

● Now place the magic wand in a pocket and, as you do so, drop the coin surreptitiously into the pocket.

● COIN FOLD

A quick and easy trick, particularly suitable for a young audience.

Effect

The performer makes a coin disappear from a folded paper.

Equipment

A 15 x 15 cm (6 x 6 in) sheet of coloured paper and a medium- to large-sized coin.

Preparation

The trick works well when making a grand show of folding the paper and sprinkling the 'magic dust'. Practise to get the paper folding just right.

Performing

● Fold the bottom edge of the paper up to about 1 cm (½ in) short of the top edge and make sure the shorter side is towards you and not the audience (**1**).

● Drop the coin into the folded paper (**2**).

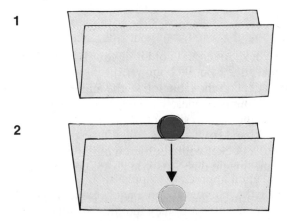

1

2

● Fold the sides of the paper towards the audience (**3**).
● Fold the top centimetre towards the audience (**4**) and
the paper will have the appearance of a secure packet,
with the coin trapped inside. In reality, the top edge of
the packet is open.

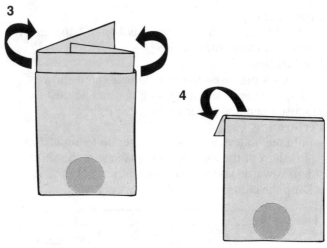

● Turn the packet over and hold it in your left hand so
that the open edge is at the bottom (**5**).
● Tap the packet on the table top so the audience can
hear that the coin is inside.
● Now allow the coin to slip out of the packet and palm
it in your left hand (**6**).
● Reach into a pocket with your left hand to pick up
some pretend 'magic dust'. As you do so, pocket the
coin.
● Pretend to sprinkle the 'magic dust' over the packet.

● Now tear up the packet. The coin has disappeared!
● Make sure you pick up the torn bits of paper
afterwards. You don't want the audience to find out
how the trick is done.

5

6

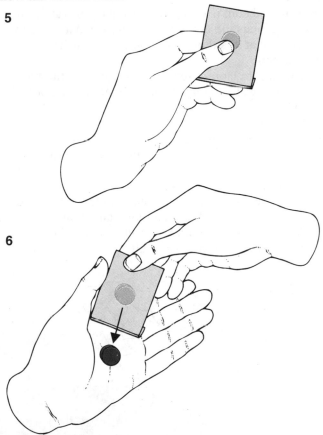

◆ THE DISSOLVING COIN

An impressive trick using several props and with
spectator participation.

Effect

A borrowed coin is dropped into a glass of water. The
audience hears the coin enter the glass and a spectator
confirms that it is there. The coin then vanishes.

Equipment

A medium- to large-sized coin, a clear glass tumbler
half full of water, a large handkerchief and an elastic
band.

Preparation

Prepare a tumbler half full of water and place an elastic
band in your left pocket. You can use a coin provided
by a spectator.

Performing

● Ask for a coin from the audience and then hold the
coin in the left hand between finger and thumb (**1**). Pick
up the handkerchief with your right hand and then
drape it over the coin in your left.

● Now hold the coin inside the handkerchief between
your right thumb and first finger (**2**), so freeing your
left hand.

● Ask a member of the audience to place the beaker in
the palm of your left hand (this also provides an
opportunity for them to check that it is an ordinary
tumbler of water).
● Hold the coin over the water with the handkerchief
draped around the glass (**3**).

● Now allow the coin to drop but before doing so secretly tilt the glass backwards so that when the coin drops it hits the side of the glass and falls into the left hand (**4**).

4

● Carefully move the glass so that it rests on top of the coin. You can now lift the handkerchief and allow someone to look straight down into the water. It appears that the coin is in the glass (**5**).

● Cover the glass again and lift it with the right hand
(**6**). The audience will now think that the coin
(supposedly inside the glass) is in your right hand. In
reality, the coin is palmed in your left hand.

● Put your left hand into your pocket to take out the
elastic band. As you do so, pocket the coin.
● Place the band around the mouth of the tumbler and
put it down on a table.

● Get a spectator – perhaps the one who provided the coin – to remove the band and handkerchief. The coin has disappeared!

● While the audience's attention is concentrated on the spectator with the glass, palm the coin. You can now make the coin appear from some other place – perhaps from behind the spectator's ear.

✖ SILVER AND COPPER

A slick trick, using more advanced moves, and suitable for doing near the middle of a magic routine. Make up your own patter and gags to make this trick truly your own.

Effect

The performer makes a silver coin and a copper coin change places.

Equipment

Three medium- to large-sized coins: two identical copper-coloured ones and a silver-coloured one of slightly different size. You will need a jacket, shirt or blouse with a wide, right pocket.

Preparation

You will need to practise until you can tell the difference between a copper and a silver coin by touch alone. The normal finger- and thumbpalms will need to be practised carefully. You need to start the trick with the three coins in a right pocket.

Performing

● Put your right hand into your pocket and as you do so, fingerpalm one of the copper coins. Do this by bending the second and third fingers around the coin in a natural manner (**1**).

● Now take the two remaining coins between your thumb and first finger and show them to the audience (**2**).

● Place the silver coin to your left and the copper one to your right on a table in front of you (**3**).

● Pick up the silver coin with your right fingers, saying you will hold it in your left hand.

● As you move to pass the silver coin from right hand to left, switch the silver coin for the copper one so that the copper coin is surreptitiously passed across. This switch is done by dropping the silver coin into your palm at the same moment as you tip the palmed copper coin into your left hand (**4**).

4

● Hold the silver coin in the palm of your right hand (**5**).

5

● Pick up the copper coin on the table with your right
fingertips and as you do so, thumbpalm the coin (**6**).
● Now tell the spectators to watch carefully.
● With hands well apart, form two fists and tap these on
the table as though in a magic gesture. The audience
now expects to see a silver coin in your left hand and a
copper coin in your right hand.
● Uncurl the fingers of your left hand to leave behind a
copper coin on the table top.
● Release the silver coin from the palm of your right
hand and leave the coin on the table. The silver and
copper coins have miraculously changed places!
● Scoop up the two coins and return them (together
with the thumbpalmed copper coin) to your pocket.

6

◆ COIN IN THE WOOL

A nice twist on the disappearing coin trick and one which involves a member of the audience.

Effect

The performer makes a coin disappear and then reappear from the centre of a ball of wool.

Equipment

A medium-sized coin, a coloured or patterned medium-sized beaker, adhesive tape, at least 10 m (40 ft) of fluffy coloured wool and an 8 x 3.5 cm (3 x 1.5 in) sheet of thin card matching the colour of the wool.

Preparation

Prepare the ball of wool in the following manner. Take the sheet of card and roll it into a tube that is 3.5 cm (1.5 in) long and has an internal diameter of 2.5 cm (1 in). Tape the end of the card to secure the tube (**1**).

1

2.5 cm

3.5 cm

Hold the tube on your thumb and carefully wind the wool around the tube to form a ball. Don't wind too tightly. Make sure that you leave one end of the tube protruding very slightly from the wool (**2**). Tuck the end of the wool into the ball.

Arrange the ball of wool in the top of the beaker with

2

the tube end pointing downwards so that the tube is not visible to the audience (**3**).

3

Performing
● Bring out the beaker and wool and place them on a table in front of the audience.
● Ask a member of the audience for a coin (make sure that you get a coin which will be small enough to fit inside the tube you have constructed).
● Get the person to mark the coin in some way, or note its date, so that he can make sure that it is his coin that he gets back again.

● Hold the coin up to the audience and then use a thumbpalm (see Silver and Copper, p. 62) to make the coin disappear.

● Now say that you will look for the missing coin. Pick up the wool with your left hand and place the wool in your right hand, putting the open end of the tube directly over the palmed coin (**4**). This frees your left hand to lift the beaker.

4

● Take the beaker in your left hand and turn it upside down to demonstrate that it is empty. At the same time, turn your right hand over so that the coin drops into the tube.

● Put the beaker down on the table right way up and take the wool in your left hand. As you do so, stick your right thumb into the tube and pull it out of the wool and palm it in your right hand (**5**).

● Direct the audience's attention to the ball of wool in your left hand. Squeeze the ball of wool to close up the opening, so keeping the coin inside.

● Place the ball of wool back on the beaker and start to

5

unravel the end of the wool from the ball.
● Invite the person who gave you the coin to pull gently
on the end of the wool and so unravel the ball. Stand
back and casually put your hands in your pockets and
so pocket the paper tube. As the spectator unwinds the
wool, the coin drops into the glass (**6**). He picks up the
coin. It is his own. How did it get there?

6

◆ TOP POCKET VANISH

A good trick to confuse people who think a vanished
coin must be hidden in one or other hand.

Effect

The performer makes a coin disappear.

Equipment

A medium- to large-sized coin and a jacket, shirt or
blouse with a top pocket containing a handkerchief.

Preparation

You will need to practise the thumbpalm (see Silver and
Copper, p. 62). A handkerchief placed in the top pocket
will hold the pocket open ready to receive the coin.

Performing

● Hold the coin in your right hand between first and
second fingers (**1**).

● Now slightly cup your left hand as if you are going to
take the coin in it. Put your right fingers into your left
hand and thumbpalm the coin in your right hand while
hidden by your left (**2**). Move your left hand away as if
it has the coin.

● Now with your right hand point and show how you will make the coin go up your left arm, across your chest, and down your right arm to your right hand (**3**).

● As your right hand passes your top pocket, drop the coin into it (**4**). Do this smoothly without any pause in your movement or explanation.

4

● Now pretend to make the coin move as you described earlier. Follow its supposed path with your eyes.
● Open your right hand. Look puzzled. The coin is not there.
● Spectators will probably assume that the coin is still in your left hand. Open that hand too. The coin has vanished!

✖ COIN THROUGH THE HANDKERCHIEF
A more advanced trick suitable for doing near the middle of a magic routine. Make up your own patter and gags to divert the audience.
Effect
The performer makes a coin appear to pass right through a handkerchief.

Equipment
A medium- to large-sized coin and a thick linen
handkerchief.
Preparation
The trick depends on the use of a sleight of hand called
the fingerpalm which, together with the patter needed to
divert the audience's interest, needs to be practised
thoroughly. Practise the sleight of hand on its own first,
together with the transfer of the coin from right to left
hand, and back again.
Performing
● Pick up the handkerchief and show it to the audience
to indicate that there is no hole in the fabric.
● Hold the handkerchief in your left hand and then pick
up the coin with your right. Hold it up between the
thumb and first two fingers of your right hand.
● With your left hand, drape the handkerchief over the
coin. There is a bump where the coin is (**1**).

1

● Take the bump with your left hand. As you do so, drop the coin into the fingers of your right hand (**2**). Grasp the bump as though the coin is still there.
● Lift the handkerchief off your right hand, still gripping the bump, but actually leaving the coin in your right hand (**3**).

● Lay the handkerchief on your right palm, on top of the coin that is hidden there. The audience should still be thinking that the bump in the handkerchief contains the coin.

● Pass your left hand back towards you close under your right hand, taking the coin from your right hand (**4**).

● Grip the handkerchief with your left hand. Pretend to squeeze the coin out through the end of the handkerchief with your right hand (**5**).

4

5

● Under the handkerchief, transfer the coin from your left hand to your right. Let the coin gradually emerge from below the bump as though it has passed through the material (**6**).

6

2. Silk and handkerchief magic

Magic tricks using handkerchiefs or silk scarfs provide
a strong visual element to a performance. These props
can be easily secreted away in a small space and
provide a dramatic flourish when they are produced.
Silk handkerchiefs and scarfs can be compressed to a
tiny size. Linen handkerchiefs, being thicker and less
supple, can be used to create shapes and hide small
objects. Whether silk or linen, scarfs and handkerchiefs
provide a very effective means of masking a magician's
moves as he or she manipulates objects 'under cover'.
Some tricks, such as The Invisible Thread (see p. 82),
Handkerchief Cleaver (see p. 88) and Blow That Knot
Away (see p. 99) require no other props and so can be
done almost anytime and anywhere. Other tricks, such
as Handkerchief In A Glass (see p. 90) and The Inner
Tube (see p. 102), require several props and can
provide a dramatic climax to a magic routine.

● PRODUCING A HANDKERCHIEF

Tricks involving the use of a handkerchief (or scarf) can be enhanced if the handkerchief is produced magically at the beginning of the trick.

Effect

A handkerchief is produced from the performer's apparently empty hands.

Equipment

A large silk handkerchief or silk scarf.

Preparation

● Lay out a handkerchief flat on a table and fold the four corners into its middle (**1**) to form a smaller square.

● Holding the corners in place, fold the new corners into the middle of the handkerchief (**2**) to form an even smaller square.

● Continue folding in this way until the handkerchief becomes very small.

1   2

● Place the folded handkerchief on your left sleeve, at the inside of the elbow joint, and hide it by pulling a fold of your sleeve over it (**3**).

● Bend your arm slightly to hold the handkerchief in position.

Performing

● Approach your audience and show them that your hands are empty.

● Put your right hand on your left sleeve and the left hand on the right as if to pull up the sleeves.

● As you do so, take hold of the hidden handkerchief in your right hand, being careful to keep it concealed.

● Put both your hands together and, using your thumbs to unfold the handkerchief, cause it to appear slowly (**4**).

● THE BOW AND ARROW HANKIE

More of a novelty than a trick. You can teach this one to a young audience.

Effect

The performer's hankie shoots from the hand, like an arrow from a bow.

Equipment

A large linen handkerchief. Use a plain-coloured one which is clean and ironed.

Preparation

This feat depends on the precise timing of the release of the left hand and the flicking action of the right. You may find the moves easier to perform using the opposite hand.

Performing

One approach is to ask the audience whether anyone has ever played bows and arrows with a hankie. If they have, get them to show how. Give them your hankie to demonstrate. If they then proceed to show you their trick, that is fine. Congratulate them and show them how *you* do it. You could even make it into a little competition. At the very least you will have grabbed the audience's attention and hopefully got them on your side. This is how you make a hankie into a bow and arrow.

● Hold the handkerchief by the opposite corners between index finger and thumb (**1**).

● Twirl the handkerchief between your hands so that it wraps around itself like a gnarled twig (**2**).

● Now turn the wrist of your right hand so that you are holding one end of the hankie as you would a bow or catapult (**3**).

● At the same time, extend your right arm and bend

back your left so that you are in a similar position to an archer drawing a bow, but with the right arm bent rather than straight.

● Increase the tension on the taut hankie as you move both hands back slightly.

● Release the hankie with your left hand a fraction of a
second before you snap your right wrist and arm
forwards and let the hankie go. The hankie will shoot
forwards across the room (**4**).

● With practice you will be able to name a target and
then hit it. The hankie can be made to travel 4–5 m
(12–15 ft) in a straight line.
● This feat is impressive to a young audience. You can
choose whether or not to show them how to do it.

● THE INVISIBLE THREAD

A charming and deceptively simple trick to entrance a
young audience.
Effect
The performer attaches an invisible thread to the centre
of the handkerchief. By pulling on the thread, the
performer makes the hankie bend back and forth. The
performer bites the magic thread in two, and the hankie

no longer moves when the thread is pulled. The hankie is then shaken open and given to the audience for examination.

Equipment

A large linen handkerchief. Use a plain-coloured one which is clean and ironed.

Preparation

Practise in front of the mirror to make sure that your thumb movements will not be detected. Presentation is all in this trick. It can be done in mime, with no speech.

Performing

● Hold the hankie in your left hand and pull it through the open fist of your right hand so that it stands upright (**1**).

● Pluck an 'invisible' thread from midair and then
pretend to pass it through the tip of the hankie and tie it.
● Now pretend to pull on the thread and, as you do so,
bend the hankie towards you (**2**) by moving your right
thumb down slightly against your fingers. This move
will be shielded by the hankie.

● Move your left hand slightly towards the hankie, and
as you do so, move your hidden right thumb up against
your fingers. The hankie will stand up.
● Repeat this back and forth pulling effect several times
to give the appearance that the hankie really is
connected to your hand by a thread.
● Now pretend to bite the thread joining your left hand
to the hankie. When you pull on the invisible thread
now, keep the hankie still.
● Shake open the hankie and hand it to a member of the
audience. 'Where is the thread?' they will wonder.

● THE BROKEN MATCH

An easy trick involving a member of the audience.

Effect

A member of the audience places a match on a handkerchief. The hankie is folded and the person is invited to break the match in half inside the handkerchief. This done, the performer makes a magic gesture or incantation and lifts up the hankie. The match falls out – it is unbroken.

✚ Equipment

A large white linen handkerchief, clean and ironed, with a match placed in its hem. A box of matches in case no members of the audience have a match.

Preparation

Open up the hem at one corner of the handkerchief and insert a match (**1**). Fold the handkerchief and place it in a top or side pocket ready for use.

Performing

● Take out the handkerchief from your pocket. Hold it up and show both sides to the audience.

● Spread the handkerchief on the table with the hidden match at the top left corner, towards the audience.

● Invite someone to throw a match into the centre of the handkerchief (provide a match if none of the audience has one).

● Fold the handkerchief (**2**) in half over the match (**a**), then quarters (**b**), then eighths (**c**) and finally sixteenths (**d**). The spectator's match will now lie along one edge of the folded handkerchief.

● Invite a member of the audience to come up and break the match in two. As you say this, move your fingers to locate the matchstick in the hem of the handkerchief. Fold this corner up to the centre of the handkerchief, making sure the audience cannot see this move.

● Hand the handkerchief to the audience member so that she picks it up from the centre where the hidden matchstick is. She will now proceed to break the concealed matchstick.

● Thank her for her help and then make a magic gesture or use a special phrase intended to mend the broken matchstick.

● Shake out the handkerchief and the apparently restored match will fall to the table.

● Hold up the handkerchief and show both sides to the audience as you did at the beginning, and then pocket the handkerchief.

Note: Don't forget to replace the broken matchstick with a fresh one before you perform the trick again.

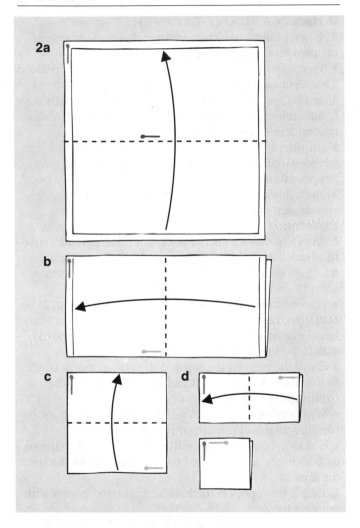

● HANDKERCHIEF CLEAVER

The performer can either perform this trick on one of his own legs or on a spectator's arm.

Effect

The performer securely knots a handkerchief or scarf around a spectator's arm. The performer then pulls the handkerchief or scarf straight through the spectator's arm with the knot still intact.

Equipment

A very large handkerchief or a square silk scarf.

Preparation

Thoroughly practise making the loop folds to give the appearance of tying a knot.

Performing

● After choosing a spectator on whom to perform your illusion, diagonally roll up the handkerchief or scarf into a rope-like length. Place it on top of the spectator's arm (**1**).

● Pretend to tie the ends below the arm in a knot (**2**) but actually take both ends of the handkerchief, form two loops just beneath the arm and fold them together (**3**).

● Pull the loops tight (**4**).

● Carry the ends to the top and then tie as many knots as you like (**5**). The handkerchief will appear to be firmly tied around the spectator's arm.

● With a magic password, grasp the knotted ends of the handkerchief and tug upwards. Underneath the spectator's arm the loops will give way and it will look as though the handkerchief has passed straight through the arm.

● Take a bow, pocket the handkerchief and get on with the next trick.

● HANDKERCHIEF IN A GLASS

This simple trick can be performed with music in the
background or you can tell an amusing story while
performing it. A little flair and showmanship will
enhance the overall effect.

Effect

A handkerchief 'escapes' through the bottom of a
sealed glass as the performer talks about escapology.

Equipment

A glass or plastic tumbler, a square silk scarf large
enough to completely cover the tumbler, two silk
handkerchiefs of different colours, cotton thread
20–25 cm (8–10 in) in length, and a medium-sized
rubber band.

Preparation

Take the handkerchief that is going to escape and tie the
cotton to one of its corners. Knot the thread at the other
end.

Performing

● Explain to the audience that you are setting out to
become an escapologist but you have decided to
practise on scarfs before trying it out on yourself.

● Put the first handkerchief (**a**) into the tumbler. Ensure
that the cotton is hanging outside the glass (**1**) on the
side facing you (and ensure that this is the side facing
you throughout the trick).

● Put the second handkerchief (**b**) on top of the first in
the glass.

● Place the scarf over the top of the glass so that it and
its contents are concealed.

● Secure the scarf with a rubber band near the rim of
the glass (**2**). Ensure that the rubber band isn't too tight.

● Turn the glass upside down to show that everything is held in place by the band. Tell the audience that it is impossible for the first handkerchief (**a**) to 'escape' from the glass.

● Utter a magic password, pull the knotted end of the cotton and handkerchief (**a**) will be pulled out of the glass (**3**).

● Take hold of the corner of handkerchief (**a**) and pull it into view. It will look as though you are pulling it through the bottom of the glass (**4**), leaving handkerchief (**b**) and the scarf in place.

● IT TIES ITSELF IN A KNOT

A simple but visually effective trick to show the power the performer has over inanimate objects.

Effect

Holding one corner of a handkerchief and letting the rest dangle, the performer lifts up the opposite corner with her other hand and gives the handkerchief a

downward shake. She tries this two or three more times
until, magically, a knot appears in the dangling corner
of thc handkerchief.

Equipment

A large handkerchief.

Preparation

Tie a knot in a corner of the handkerchief.

Performing

● Tell the audience that you will make a handkerchief
tie itself in a knot just by using a sharp flick of your
wrist.

● Take the knotted corner of the handkerchief, hiding
the knot in your cupped right hand (**1**).

● With your left hand, bring thc dangling opposite
corner up and grasp it with the thumb and first finger of
your right hand.

● Give the handkerchief a sharp downward shake, releasing the untied end as you do so. It will appear to the audience that you have failed in your intention to make the handkerchief tie itself (**2**). Seem puzzled by the handkerchief's failure to obey your will.

● Repeat these actions twice more, the left hand always bringing the untied corner up to the right one.

● On the final shake, retain the untied corner between your thumb and first finger but open your other fingers to release the knotted end (**3**). It will look as though, after two attempts, the handkerchief has obliged you by tying itself in a knot.

● IT WAS A KNOT BUT NOW IT'S NOT

A truly illusive trick requiring rudimentary sleight of hand.

Effect

After allowing two coloured silk handkerchiefs to be closely examined by a spectator, the performer throws them into the air: the handkerchiefs come down tied together. The knotted handkerchiefs are thrown upwards a second time and, when they return to earth, they are no longer tied to one another.

Equipment

Two large, coloured handkerchiefs (preferably of silk) and a very small, thin flesh-coloured rubber band.

Preparation

There is none apart from some practice, so that the performer's actions might be as smooth as possible.

Performing

● Place the rubber band over the first finger and thumb of the same hand, keeping them very close together (**1**).

● With your other hand, pick up the two handkerchiefs and ask the spectator to examine them closely.

● When the spectator hands back the handkerchiefs, ensure that you take each by a corner and put them between the first finger and thumb, above the rubber band (**2**).

● Stand so that your handkerchief-holding hand is furthest away from the audience.

● Drop your hand slightly and allow the rubber band to slip from your hand onto the ends of the handkerchiefs (**3**).

● Throw the handkerchiefs into the air. They will seem to be tied together as they land.

● Carefully pick up one handkerchief by its corner, so
that the audience can see that the other is hanging from
it, as if they were tied together.

● Throw the tied handkerchiefs into the air and give the
one you are holding a sharp tug just as it leaves your
hand. This will pull the handkerchiefs apart.

● As they float downwards, the audience will see that
the handkerchiefs are no longer 'knotted' together.

● PEN THROUGH HANDKERCHIEF

This is a simple and visually effective trick.

Effect

The performer borrows a spectator's handkerchief and
seems to make a pen pass right through it without
damaging the handkerchief.

Equipment

A borrowed handkerchief and a pen or pencil.

Preparation

It is the presentation and patter that bring this trick to
life.

Performing

● Ask a spectator for a large handkerchief.

● Hold your left hand out, keeping your left elbow
against your body. Draw attention to this hand as you
close it to make a fist (**1**).

● Place the borrowed handkerchief over your fist.

● Now that your fist is hidden, open it as though
holding a beaker (**2**).

● With your right thumb facing downward, bring your
right hand against the handkerchief, moving the thumb

into your left hand, thereby creating a vertical fold (**3**).

● Enclose your right thumb with your left hand, at the same time moving your hands towards your body, so that both thumbs face your body.

● Once you've finished this action, move your right thumb up and down a couple of times and then remove it, leaving your left hand where it is. You have created a vertical fold, although it will appear to the audience that you have created a dead-end depression by pushing the middle of the handkerchief into your fist.

● Take the pen, push it into the depression (really the fold) and move it up and down a couple of times, pretending that you are having some difficulty in making it penetrate the handkerchief.

● On the last attempt, push the pen halfway down, then hit the top of the pen with the palm of your right hand to force it down into the fold (**4**).

● Move your right hand under your left fist and pull the pen through the fold (**5**).

● To show that the handkerchief is unharmed, open up your left fist beneath it and turn the palm upwards. The secret fold will drop out because of this action.

4

5

◆ BLOW THAT KNOT AWAY

A rather elegant trick that involves some nimble finger play.

Effect

A knot is tied in the middle of a large handkerchief. The performer blows on the knot and it vanishes.

Equipment

A large linen or silk handkerchief.

Preparation

The twist of the wrist as the knot is tied needs to be practised as a smooth movement that conceals the trickery.

Performing

● Diagonally roll up the handkerchief and present it to your audience, holding it at the ends.

● Hold end (**a**) between the first and second fingers of your left hand, with the third and fourth fingers curled around the handkerchief (**1**).

● Hold end (**b**) between the first and second fingers of your right hand.

● Your palms should face upwards and both ends of the handkerchief should extend about 8 cm (3 in) beyond the hands.

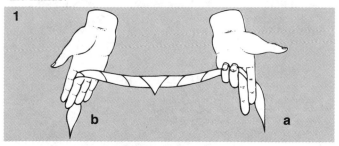

● Place end **(b)** in your left hand, so that it is held between the base of your left first finger and thumb (**2**).
● Reach through the loop from above and, using your right thumb and first finger, take hold of end **(a)** (**3**).
● Bring end **(a)** through the loop, turning your left hand so that your fingertips point downwards as you do so, allowing your left second finger to catch in the knot and form a smaller loop in the handkerchief (**4**). Don't let the audience know that you've sabotaged your knot in this way.

● Tighten the knot and slip your finger out of it as you do so.

● Hold the handkerchief in your left hand, showing the knot to the audience, and then press down on the knot with your right hand, so loosening it (**5**).

● Keep holding the knot in your right hand and place the topmost corner of the handkerchief over your right first finger.

● Release your right hand's pressure on the knot as you blow on it (**6**). It will look as though you have blown that knot away!

✖ THE INNER TUBE

An impressive trick that can provide a stunning climax
to a performance.

Effect

The performer shows the audience two hollow tubes –
one inside the other. From these apparently empty
tubes, the performer produces several silk scarfs, and
then, as a finale, a wine glass.

✚ Equipment

Three large cardboard or plastic tubes of similar height
and slightly differing diameters (dried skimmed milk
and drinking chocolate containers or similar are
suitable). Black paint and a paintbrush. Scissors or a
modelling knife, straight edge and cutting board. Two
sheets of brightly coloured, sticky-backed paper. A
10 cm (4 in) length of wire bent into a narrow U-shape.
Adhesive tape. Three silk scarfs and a wine glass.

Preparation

Remove the ends from the two largest diameter tubes.
Keep the base of the smallest diameter tube in place
(**1**). Trim the three tubes so that the largest diameter
tube (**a**) is 3 cm (1¼ in) taller than the second-widest
tube (**b**), which in turn is 3 cm (1¼ in) taller than the
narrowest tube (**c**). Take tubes (**a**) and (**b**) and coat their
insides with black paint and their outsides with brightly
coloured paper of differing colour or design. Use
adhesive tape to attach the bent wire securely inside the
open end of tube (**c**) and then paint both the inside and
outside black, ensuring that the wire and tape are also
painted.

In preparation for the trick, place the wine glass and three scarfs inside tube (**c**). Then hook the tube inside tube (**b**) and place the two inside tube (**a**) (**2**). Ideally, place the tubes on the table where you intend to perform.

Performing

● At the start of the trick, lift up tube (**a**) and turn it towards the audience to show that it is empty (**3**).

● Explain that one tube fits snugly inside the other and that tube too is empty. As you say this, put tube (**a**) down and then pick up tube (**b**) (with tube (**c**) hidden inside) and put it inside tube (**a**) (**4A**).

● As you do this, make sure that the hook on tube (**c**) catches the lip of tube (**a**).

● Lift up tube (**a**) and tube (**c**) will come with it (**4B**). With the other hand you can lift up tube (**b**) and show the audience that it too is empty.

● Now place the middle tube (**b**) on the table and set the largest one (**a**) over it so that the smallest, hidden tube (**c**) is nesting in the middle (**4C**).

● Make a magic incantation or gesture and then produce the items you have previously loaded, starting with the scarfs and finishing with the wine glass.

● Take a bow and expect applause. You deserve it.

3. String and rope magic

Tricks using string or rope are very popular and many professional magicians include at least one in their performances. The presentation of such tricks needs to be thought through carefully, because the audience needs to be close enough to see the cleverness of the trick, but not too close (or in the wrong place) so that they can see how the trick is done. Rope tricks, like most other forms of magic, have been with us for a very long time.

Use soft and supple white rope or cord, or large white shoelaces. These are much more pliable than ordinary rope or string and their light colour means they show up well. Even easier to perform with is proper magician's rope, available from most magic shops.

Practise rope tricks so that your movements are smooth, and your hands relaxed, with no hint of clumsiness. Timing is important, and you need to pace the trick carefully, so that the early stages are slow and deliberate while later stages, where the trickery occurs, are faster and build up to a climax.

Some rope tricks, such as Impossible Release (see p. 116) and A Mug's Game (see p. 129), can be done on quite a grand scale and involve several people. Others, such as Instant Knot (opposite) or Vanishing Knots (see p. 111), can be performed almost anywhere and require no equipment other than a length of rope or string.

● **INSTANT KNOT**

Less of a trick and more of a novelty. You tie a knot in record time!

Effect

The performer shows the unknotted string to the audience. She brings her hands together and a knot appears instantaneously.

Equipment

A 1.3 m (4 ft) length of string.

Preparation

A quick and easy trick requiring no special preparation.

Performing

● Hand the string to a member of the audience so that he can check there are no knots in it. Take back the string.

● Hold the string with the left hand, palm up, about 15 cm (6 in) from end (**a**) and with the right hand, palm down, about 15 cm (6 in) from end (**b**) (**1**). Hand position is crucial.

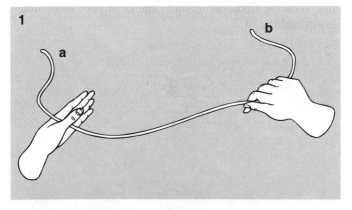

● Now, turn the right-hand palm towards you, with the fingers going under the string (**2**).

● Explain, 'I will now try to break the world record for tying an overhand knot. Ready! Steady! Go!' Bring your hands together quickly.
● Bring your right hand behind the left and with the first and second fingers of your right hand grasp end (**a**). With the first and second fingers of your left hand grasp end (**b**) (**3**).

● Move your hands apart and when you pull the string taut, a knot appears instantly in its centre (**4**).

● ONE-HANDED INSTANT KNOT

One better than the previous trick. You tie the knot with one hand!

Effect

The performer shows the unknotted string to the audience. He holds the string in one hand, shakes the rope slightly, and a knot appears.

Equipment

A 1.3 m (4 ft) length of string.

Preparation

A quick and easy trick requiring little preparation. Practise until you can do the moves quickly and smoothly.

Performing

● Hand the string to a member of the audience so that she can check there are no knots in it.

● Hold the rope in your right hand (or left) so that it passes between the second and third fingers and over the thumb (**1**). End (**a**) should hang down about 25 cm (10 in).

● Now turn your right (or left) hand towards you and grasp end (**a**) between thumb and forefinger (**2**).

● Shake your hand so that the loop around the hand falls off and passes over end (**a**). A knot forms (**3**) and the audience is truly mystified.

◆ **VANISHING KNOTS**

A good effect to follow the Instant Knot or the One-Handed Instant Knot.

Effect

The performer shows a knotted string to the audience and then adds one knot and then another. When a volunteer pulls on the ends of the string, the knots fall apart.

Equipment

A 1.3 m (4 ft) length of string.

Preparation

Practise this trick so as to aim for as much audience participation as possible. The string should have a half-hitch knot in it (**1**), as formed using the Instant Knot (see p. 107) or the One-Handed Instant Knot (see p. 109).

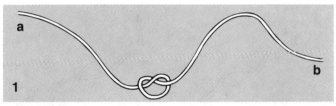

Performing

● Hand the knotted string to a member of the audience to check.

● Explain, 'The easiest way to undo a knot is to tie a couple more.'

● Holding the string up so the audience can see, tie another half-hitch in the string to form a reef knot (**2**) (see overleaf). Do not pull the ends too tight, but leave the loops of the knot open slightly.

• Continue, 'Now we join the two parts of this knot with a third knot.' As you say this, push end (**a**) through the lower loop from the far side (**3**).
• Now push end (**a**) through the top loop, again from the far side (**4**).

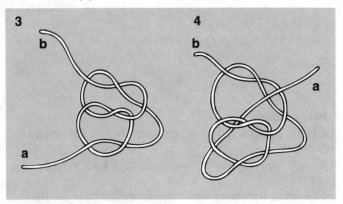

• Ask a member of the audience to gently pull on the two ends of the string. When he does this the knots get smaller and smaller and then fall apart.

◆ MAGIC SCISSORS

Performed slowly, the trick is clever, performed quickly it is magical.

Effect

The performer threads a string through the handle of a pair of scissors. She then invites a member of the audience to release the scissors without breaking the string and with another member of the audience holding the string by its ends. The volunteer does not succeed. The performer then shows him how.

Equipment

A 2 m (6 ft) length of string. A pair of large scissors with fully looped handles.

Preparation

A straightforward trick. No special preparation is required, although if you plan to do the quick version of the trick, you need to practise it rigorously.

Performing

● Fold the piece of string at its centre and push this loop through one handle of the pair of scissors (**1**).

1

● Put both ends of the string through the central loop and then through the other handle (**2**).

2

● Pull the ends of the string to form a neat arrangement and show the scissors and string to the audience (**3**).

3

● Ask a volunteer to hold the ends of the string and then get another volunteer to see whether he can release the scissors without breaking the string and with the other person holding the string by its ends. It is very unlikely that he will succeed.

● Take back the scissors and string and then proceed to show them how it is done. Note: If the neat arrangement has been altered, you may need to rearrange or even rethread the string. If so, show the arrangement to the audience to show that you are not cheating.

● Get the first volunteer to hold the ends of the string.

● The next part you can do slowly, explaining as you go, or quickly, without explanation, for a more dramatic effect.

● Pull the central loop out and pass it through the other handle of the scissors (**4**).

4

● Next, being careful not to twist the loop, open it out further, and then pass the loop right over the scissors (**5**).

5

● Now ask the volunteer to pull gradually on the ends of the string. The string will unthread itself from the scissors and come free!

◆ IMPOSSIBLE RELEASE
An impressive feat of escapology with plenty of audience involvement. It is particularly suitable for a young audience.
Effect
A scarf is tied around the performer's wrists and a rope then threaded around the scarf. Another scarf is draped over her wrists and in less than a minute she releases herself from the rope.
Equipment
A 4 m (12 ft) length of soft rope and two large silk scarfs.

Preparation

Make sure the props you need are placed on a table ready for use. The trick works particularly well if you grab the audience's attention by telling them an escapology story while freeing yourself from the rope.

Performing

● Get a spectator to check that the rope you are using is strong and that there is nothing unusual about it.

● Meanwhile, get a second spectator to tie your wrists together with one of the scarfs. Keep your fists closed while this is being done.

● Ask the first spectator to pass the rope between your wrists (**1**) and then get him to keep hold of both ends of the rope.

● Now get the second spectator to drape the other scarf over your wrists.

● Open your hands and pull backwards slightly. As you do so, explain that the rope is secure around your tied wrists. Pulling backwards will have brought the rope hard against the tied scarf.

● Begin telling the story of Harry Houdini, the great
escapologist, his feats and how he died (see p. 11).
While doing this, open your hands and rub the heel of
one hand against the other to trap and then move the
rope towards your palms (**2**).

● As you continue talking, make a step towards the
spectator holding the rope. As the rope slackens, work
your hands backwards and forwards until you can bend
your fingers and slip the loop over one hand (**3**).

● Now ask the spectator to pull the rope taut. As he does so, the rope will be drawn beneath the scarf and come free.

● Ask the volunteer to remove the scarf draped over your wrists. This exposes the other scarf which is still securely tied in place.

● Get the volunteer to undo the silk around your wrists. Then take your bow.

◆ RING RELEASE
A neat trick that will perplex your audience.
Effect
The performer threads a small ring onto a length of string. Two spectators each hold one end of the string, with the ring hanging at the centre. A handkerchief is then thrown over the ring and the performer places his hands beneath the handkerchief. Seconds later the handkerchief is removed to reveal the ring secured in place by a matchstick. A spectator removes the matchstick and the ring falls to the ground free of the string.
✦ Equipment
A 1.5 m (5 ft) length of string. Two identical metal or plastic rings of about 2.5 cm (1 in) diameter. A matchstick, a silk handkerchief and a wristwatch.
Preparation
Use a thumbpalm as described in Top Pocket Vanish (see p. 70) to hide one of the rings in your left hand. Hide the matchstick beneath your wristwatch (**1**) (see overleaf).

1

Performing
● Ask one of the spectators to check the string, the ring (not the hidden one!) and the handkerchief.
● Thread the visible ring onto the string and then get two spectators to hold either end of the string.
● Move the ring to the centre of the string and then place the handkerchief over it (**2**).

● Explain that you are just going to check everything is OK. As you say this, put both hands under the handkerchief and, under cover, take out the matchstick from under your wristwatch.

● Quickly secure the palmed ring to the string using the matchstick (**3**). Put your left hand over the previously threaded ring and then remove the handkerchief.

3

● Exclaim in surprise as you notice the match threaded through the ring.

● Run your left hand (with the threaded ring concealed) along the string to the person on your left, as you ask him to remove the match. To do this he has to let go of the string and this gives you the opportunity to take your left hand (still holding the concealed ring) off the left end of the string.

● While the spectator is removing the match from the central ring, palm or pocket the other ring.

● When the match is removed the ring is released from the string. No one will be any the wiser as to how the trick is done.

● CHINESE ROBBERY

An easy trick using a volunteer and suitable for a young audience.

Effect

Six traditional Chinese coins (or metal washers) are threaded onto a string. The string is knotted and the ends tied around a person's waist. The coins (or washers) are then covered with a handkerchief. The magician, playing the part of a Chinese pickpocket, steals the money by removing it magically from the string.

Equipment

A 2 m (6 ft) length of string. Six traditional Chinese coins or metal washers. A large handkerchief.

Preparation

No special preparation is required.

Performing

● Explain, 'Until only recently, the Chinese preferred clothes without pockets. They had an unusual way of carrying loose change. They made coins with holes in the middle and carried the coins on a piece of string hanging from around the waist. Chinese pickpockets used a very cunning method to steal the coins.'

● Show the audience the coins or washers and the piece of string.

● Fold the string in half and push its centre through one of the coins (or washers). Then pass both ends of the string through the loop to secure the coin to the centre of the string (**1**).

● Continue, 'Other coins are put on top,' and saying this, thread both ends of the string through several more coins (**2**).

● Now tie a single half-hitch about 10 cm (4 in) above the coins and then tie the string loosely around the waist of one of the spectators so that the coins are hanging from his or her side (**3**).

1

2

3

● Place the handkerchief over the coins, explaining, 'This is how the coins might be carried, hidden by the handkerchief.'

● Continue, 'The amazing thing is how the pickpocket was able to remove the coins without untying or cutting the string.' Saying this, reach under the handkerchief, slide the top five coins upwards with one hand, and with the other hand loosen the securing loop and then pull it down over the remaining coin (**4**).

4

● Allow the coins to slide off the string and into your hand.

● Adding, 'And to this day, they don't know how it's done.' Whisk the handkerchief away to reveal the coins in your hand and the piece of string still intact.

◆ **CUT AND RESTORED ROPE**

A classic trick which has been popular for hundreds of years.

Effect

A length of string is cut in half by a spectator. The performer restores it into one piece.

Equipment

A 1.5 m (5 ft) length of soft rope, ideally magician's rope. A large pair of scissors.

Preparation

Plenty of practice is needed to make sure the crucial move is done smoothly and discreetly.

Performing

● Give the rope to a member of the audience to check.

● Take the rope back and then hold it between the thumb and first finger of the left hand about 3 cm (1 in) from the ends of the rope (**1**). The back of your hand should be towards the audience.

a

● With your right hand grasp the middle of the rope at point (**a**) and bring it up to your left hand (**2**).

● When (**a**) has reached your hand, without stopping pick up the rope at point (**b**) and bring the resulting loop up beside the two ends of the rope (**3**). This needs to be practised carefully, and done as one smooth movement. To the audience it will seem that you have simply picked up the centre of the rope and placed it as a loop beside the two ends.

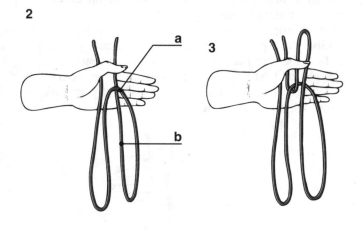

● Ask a spectator to cut through the top of the loop (**4**) making sure the arrangement of rope in your hand is well hidden.

● Next drop the two long ends (**5**). To the audience you now appear to have two roughly equal lengths of rope.

● Tie the two short ends of rope into a knot around the
the long length (**6**). Make sure you keep the knot well
shielded from the audience until it is complete.

● Now hold the rope at one end, showing that it (apparently) consists of two pieces of roughly equal length joined by a knot in the middle (**7**).

● As the finale, and in full view of the audience, take the knot gently between the thumb and forefinger of your other hand and then gently blow on the knot. As you do so, slide the knot down the longer length of rope and off the end.

7

● Throw the knot into the audience for them to examine and hold up the long length, while taking your bow.

◆ A MUG'S GAME
A platform trick with plenty of audience participation.
Effect
Two lengths of rope are tied to a wand and to each other. Then two mugs are threaded onto the ropes and two silk scarfs tied around them to anchor the ropes together. The magician removes the wand and the two ropes fall free of one another, bringing the mugs clattering to the ground.

Equipment
Two identical 4 m (12 ft) lengths of soft rope. A magic wand, two enamel coffee mugs and two silk scarfs.

Preparation
Practise a very smooth performance with plenty of patter to direct attention away from the crucial knot tied around the wand.

Performing
● Get two spectators to assist you. Place one assistant either side of you about 3 m (10 ft) apart and facing each other. Give them the two ropes to hold so that the ropes are parallel. Place the magic wand under the centre of the ropes (**1**).

● Ask the assistants to release the ropes and then get them each to hold one end of the wand (**2**). The ropes are now supported in the middle by the wand.

● Gather the two ropes together (**3**) and then explain that you will tie them both to the wand. Unknown to the audience and assistants, you tie them in such a way that they are held together by the wand (**4**).

4

• Now give two ends back to each spectator. What the assistants do not know is that the two ends they now hold each belong to the same rope (**5**). When they walk backwards to their original positions, the ropes will hang across with the wand tied in the middle.

5

● To make the trick appear more dramatic (and to add greater confusion) thread the handles of a mug through the ropes on one side and then tie a scarf around the ropes. Repeat this for the other side (**6**).

6

● Explain what you have done. You have tied the ropes to the wand and you have joined the ropes together in more than one place (point to the mugs and the scarfs). The ropes are securely held together.
● Now move to the centre of the ropes, saying, 'But now I want to get my wand back.' Put your hand over the knot and pull out your wand. The two ropes will fall free of one another with a crash as the mugs hit the ground.
● Finish with, 'It's amazing what a wand can do,' and take a bow.

✖ ROPES CHANGE LENGTH

This is one of the most impressive rope tricks to show children. It sounds complicated when you first read the instructions but it is quite easy to work out if you have the ropes in your hand and you follow the steps one at a time.

Effect

In the hands of a performer, a short, medium and long length of rope all become the same length and then revert back to their original lengths.

Equipment

Three lengths of soft rope – one 60 cm (24 in) long, a second 30 cm (12 in) long and a third 20 cm (8 in) long.

Preparation

Plenty of practice is needed to make sure you get the looping moves and the counting just right.

Performing

• Show the pieces of rope to the audience and then put them in your left hand and place them under your thumb with the back of your hand towards the audience. The longest rope (**a**)(**b**) is to the left, the medium rope (**c**)(**d**) is in the middle, and the shortest rope (**e**)(**f**) is to the right (**1**).

• Grab the bottom end (**b**)

of the long rope with your right hand and put it under
your left thumb between the top ends (**c**) and (**e**) of the
medium and short pieces (**2**).

● Take the bottom end (**d**) of the medium piece with
your right hand and put this in a position to the right of
the top end (**e**) of the short piece (**3**).

● Next, put your right hand through the loop formed by
the long piece and take the bottom end (**f**) of the short
piece and place it to the right of its other end (**e**), so that
the short rope (**e**)(**f**) loops around (**a**)(**b**) but is above
(**c**)(**d**), as shown in (**4**).

4

a c b e f d

● Now, with you right hand, pick up ends (**e**) (**f**) and (**d**) and draw these to your right, hiding the loop (**e**)(**f**) behind the fingers of your right hand. Done smoothly, the move gives the appearance that the three ropes are now all the same length (**5**).

5

e f d

right-hand thumb

left-hand thumb

a b c

● Hold the ropes in your right hand with the ends dangling down (**6**).

● To convince the audience that the three ropes really are of the same length, you count the ropes singly from hand to hand.

● Bring the right hand over to the left and transfer the medium length rope to the left hand (**7**), counting 'one' as you do so.

● Now bring your right hand back to the left again, and transfer the medium rope back to the finger and thumb of the right hand and, at the same time, pick up the looped short and long ropes between the first and second finger of the left hand, counting 'two' as you do so (**8**).

● Finally, bring your right hand back to the left once more and transfer the medium rope to the left hand, counting 'three' as you do so. You have now 'counted' the three ropes from right to left.
● Now scrunch the three ropes together in your left hand, and then slowly pull them out, one at a time, starting with the shortest and ending with the longest. Hold the ropes up as you did at the start of the trick and take a bow for your richly deserved applause.

4. Paper magic

Paper napkins, newspapers and sheets or loops of paper are light and flimsy props which lend themselves very well to a variety of tricks. The five tricks described here require some other props, and four of them require special preparation but are well worth the effort. Torn and Restored Newspaper (see p. 147) works well as a stage performance. Linking Clips (below) can be done on the spot with little or no preparation.

● LINKING CLIPS
A trick that works of its own accord.
Effect
The performer folds a piece of paper and attaches two paperclips to it. He pulls on the ends of the paper and the clips become linked together. The trick is repeated but this time using two chains of paperclips and with a volunteer holding the ends of the two chains. When the performer pulls on the ends of the paper, the two chains become magically linked in the hands of the volunteer.
Equipment
A strip of paper 15 x 7.5 cm (6 x 3 in) or a novelty banknote. Two individual paperclips and two chains of five paperclips each.
Preparation
No special preparation is needed. Make sure you have all the materials readily to hand. The two chains of paperclips are simply made by linking clips together as shown (**1**).

1

Performing

● Fold the strip of paper so that its top edge forms the
letter S and carefully attach the two paperclips to hold
the loops of the S together (**2**). The precise positioning
of the clips is important.

2

● Check that no one is standing too close (flying
paperclips are dangerous), then begin, 'Everything is
automated these days. Even paperclip joining . . .' On
saying this, pull the two ends of the paper apart
smoothly and quickly. The clips will fly off and link
themselves together.

● 'Here are two chains I did earlier,' and bring out the
two paperclip chains.

● Ask for a volunteer from the audience and get him to

hold one end of each chain while you attach the other
ends to the paper as before (**3**).

● 'It even works with chains,' and pull on the ends of
the paper. The two chains of paperclips will link
together in the hands of the volunteer.

3

● MYSTERIOUS LOOPS

This one is based on the classic trick called The Afghan
Bands. It works particularly well with older children.
There are many ways of presenting this trick. Here is
one.

Effect

The performer invites two members of the audience to
help her. She takes a loop of paper and carefully cuts
along its centre line to produce two separate loops. One
of the spectators copies her actions but ends up with a
single long loop. The second spectator follows suit. He
finishes up with two loops – but they are linked
together, not separate.

✚ Equipment

Three coloured strips of paper, say red, blue and green, each 2 m (6 ft) long and 7.5 cm (3 in) wide. Glue and a pair of sharp-pointed scissors.

Preparation

Take one strip of paper, the red (**a**), and glue the ends together without twisting the strip. Take the second strip of paper, the blue (**b**), and twist it once before joining the ends together with glue. Finally, take the third strip of paper, the green (**c**), and twist it twice before gluing the ends (**1**). Start the performance with the three loops of paper and the scissors close at hand.

1

a

b

c

Performing

● Explain to the audience that you have three magic loops that seem to have a will of their own.

● Pick up the red loop of paper and hold it high to show the audience. As you do so, explain what you are going to do. 'I am going to cut this loop of paper along its length. Let's see what happens . . .'

● Now start to cut the loop along its length but stop after a few seconds (**2**). Ask the audience, 'What do you think I will be left with when I've finished?' Listen to the various answers and look where they come from. Then continue, 'Well, let's see.'

● Continue cutting along the length of the loop and when complete you will be left with two separate loops of paper. Hold them up and show them to the audience.

● Now, seek out a member of the audience who expected you to finish up with one large loop. Ask him to come up and repeat what you did and see what happens.

● Hand him the blue loop. When he carefully cuts along its length he will be left with one large loop (**3**) – what he predicted!

3

● Continue, 'I got two separate loops. My friend here got one. Did anyone expect something different to happen?' Listen to their answers and then pick a second volunteer: 'Well, let's see what happens when you try.'
● Give him the green loop of paper. When he finishes cutting he will be left with two loops of paper – but linked together (**4**).

4

● Finish with, 'I told you so. They're magic loops. They seem to have a mind of their own!' and take a bow.

◆ A SWEET SURPRISE

A trick to be performed at the dinner table! Presented in a casual manner it will certainly take your dinner guests by surprise.

Effect

The performer takes a paper napkin from someone at the dinner table. With a pen he draws a circle and dot on a sugar cube and then drops the cube into a glass of water where it dissolves. He presses the folded napkin down on top of the glass and the circle and dot are magically transferred from the sugar cube to the napkin.

Equipment

Two identical paper napkins. A felt-tip pen, a sugar cube and a glass of water.

Preparation

Whether you perform this trick at the dinner table in your own home, or whether you perform it in a restaurant, you will need to prepare a napkin in advance (the same type of napkin that the other guests are using). Fold the napkin into four and then draw a faint circle and a dot in the centre of one side (**1**). This is the same mark that you will later draw on the sugar cube. Conceal the napkin neatly folded in a pocket until you are ready to do the trick. There needs to be a bowl of sugar cubes and a glass of water on the dinner table before you start.

Performing

● While sitting at the dinner table, secretly take out the concealed napkin and place it on your lap.

● Ask someone to pass you a clean paper napkin. Fold it carefully into four to produce a neat square (this should be similar to the paper square you have on your lap).

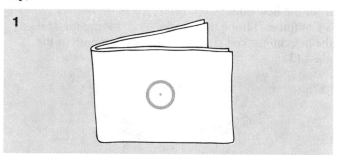

● Casually explain to the onlookers, 'I learnt this from a friend recently. It doesn't always work, but let's try it and see.'

● Take a sugar cube from the bowl and draw a circle and a dot on it (**2**).

● Hold the sugar cube in your left hand and with your attention fixed firmly on the glass of water, drop the sugar cube into the water, saying, 'Now let's see what happens.' At the same time, casually pick up the fresh napkin with your right hand and place it in your lap.

● Still with your concentration on the glass, pick up the concealed napkin with your right hand, thus exchanging it for the new one.
● Continue, 'I hope this works' and, saying this, press the napkin marked side down over the mouth of the glass (**3**).

● Keep your hand on the napkin for half a minute or so, peering into the glass as you do so and noticing the sugar cube gradually dissolve. This is the time to use your left hand to pocket the napkin which is lying on your lap.
● Finish with 'That should do it' and, saying this, lift up the napkin to show the circle and dot magically transferred to the paper.

◆ TORN AND RESTORED NEWSPAPER

An impressive trick that works on a deceptively easy principle. It depends on careful preparation and slick presentation.

Effect

A newspaper is torn into shreds and is then magically restored to its original form.

Equipment

Two copies of the *same* newspaper, a glue stick, a warm (not hot) iron and an ironing board.

Preparation

Practise by using the identical inner pages of the two newspapers. Use the cover pages of the two newspapers to perform the trick in front of the audience. The labelling below applies to the performance itself, not the practice sessions.

Take the cover pages of the two newspapers (**a**) and (**b**). On the inside front cover (page 2) of paper (**a**) apply a small patch of glue (**g**) from a glue stick (**1**).

Place paper (**b**) back-to-back with paper (**a**) so that
page 3 of paper (**b**) is stuck to page 2 of paper (**a**) (**2**).

2

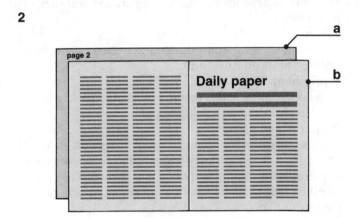

Now fold paper (**b**) in half, then in quarters (**3**), eighths,
sixteenths, and so on (**4**), until you are left with paper
(**b**) in a small bundle stuck to page 2 of paper (**a**). With
a warm (not hot) iron, press flat the bundle formed by
paper (**b**) so that it lies inconspicuously inside paper (**a**).

3

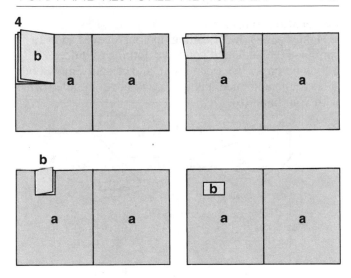

Now fold paper (**a**) so that the newspaper bundle (**b**) is inside (**5**). You are ready to perform.

Performing

● Make a big show of rolling up your sleeves so as to convince the audience you have nothing to hide.

● Pick up paper (**a**), open it out, and casually show both sides to the audience, taking care to cover bundle (**b**) with your hand (**6**).

6

● Explain to the audience that you like this trick – it allows you to rip something to pieces and it's a good way of letting off steam.

● Now tear down the centrefold of paper (**a**) and place the back page in front of the front page (**7**).

7

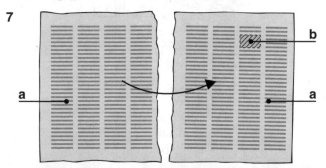

● Fold paper (**a**) across the middle and then tear it across (**8**), putting the lower half in front of the upper half.

8

● Continue folding and tearing the paper in half, each time putting the torn pieces in front, so that bundle (**b**) always stays at the back.
● When the torn paper (**a**) is only slightly larger than the bundle (**b**), place the two between your hands and turn your hands so that paper (**a**) is below bundle (**b**). With the lower hand squeeze paper (**a**) into a ball (**9**).

9

● Close your eyes and say your favourite magic word or phrase.

● Open your eyes and lift off your top hand to reveal bundle (**b**) neatly folded (**10**).

10

● Unfold bundle (**b**), a step at a time, until you reveal the double page quite restored and whole (**11**).

11

• You can even show the reverse side of the paper, with the bundle of torn bits held under your thumb. They are glued down on the bottom piece only, so make sure none fall and give the game away.

• Squeeze the whole thing into a ball and put it in your pocket or discard it safely.

◆ MAKING MONEY

This trick will have the audience eating out of your hand. It works on a similar principle to the previous trick.

Effect

The performer takes a piece of paper and folds it in half several times. When he unfolds it, the paper has changed into a banknote.

Equipment

A £10 note or a novelty banknote. A piece of paper of exactly the same size cut from a glossy magazine. A medium-sized envelope and two small pellets of Blu-Tack. A wallet or purse in your pocket.

Preparation

Lay the banknote on a table with the Queen or face side face up. Fold the note in half (**1**) and then in half again

1

(**2**) and then fold the lower half upwards (**3**).
Now do exactly the same with the glossy paper. Stick
two small pieces of Blu-Tack to the paper (**4**). Now turn
the banknote upside down with respect to the glossy
paper and stick the two folded pieces of paper together
(**5**).

Now unfold the glossy paper (with the folded banknote
attached to its back) and place it in an envelope with
the banknote side face down (**6**). You are ready to
perform the trick.

6

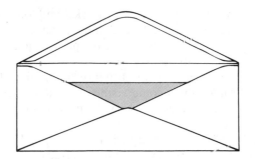

Performing

● Pick up the envelope and explain to the audience, 'I got this in the post the other day from a magician. It's a magic piece of paper. He said I'd make a lot of money from it.'

● Take out the paper, taking care to keep your left hand obscuring the folded banknote (**7**). Show the paper to the audience.

7

● Continue, 'He told me how it works' and, on saying this, fold the paper in half, and in half again, in exactly the same way as you did during the preparation. The previous folds will guide you.

● When the paper is small, turn it over, and the £10 note will suddenly become visible. Unfold the banknote slowly, taking care not to show the now hidden paper to the audience.

● Finally, when the banknote is fully unfolded, pull it away from the paper so that it breaks free of the Blu-Tack.

● Take the banknote in one hand, and keeping the paper concealed in the other, hold the banknote up to the light to check that it is real.

● While you are doing this, and with your eyes fixed on the banknote, reach into a pocket with your other hand to take out your purse or wallet. As you do so, pocket the piece of paper.

● Take out the purse or wallet and put the banknote inside it saying something like, 'If I carry on making money like this, I'll be able to retire early.'

5. Mind magic

Entertainers who perform mind magic, or mentalism, claim to use special mental powers to perform apparently superhuman feats. Such demonstrations include predicting the future, reading people's minds (telepathy) and matching an object to a person (psychometry). In a performance of mental magic much depends on the magician's ability to convey a sense of mystery and wonder. Although some magicians specialize in this kind of magic to the exclusion of all else – and they cultivate unusual looks or behaviour to distinguish them from other performers – just one or two mentalist items in your performance can do much to enhance your reputation.

There are some specific points to consider when performing mind magic. Use the word 'test' or 'experiment' rather than 'trick' to describe what you are doing. This reinforces the idea that you are using special powers, not a conjuring trick, to achieve a particular effect. Do not invent complicated explanations for your powers – it is better to simply leave it as a mysterious process. If a coincidence or unusual event happens, claim, with a knowing smile or wink, that you might have planned it all along. Be slightly wrong now and then. Making a guess which is nearly right, but not quite, adds authenticity and helps make the audience believe than you trying to 'read people's minds'. Use everyday items, rather than special props, to help maintain the idea that it is you, not the props, that are special. Most mentalist feats

depend on knowledge about how the human mind
works but also use simple conjuring principles to
produce an effect. Try these tricks and see for yourself.
Some are truly mind-boggling.

● RIGHT EVERY TIME

A quick and easy first trick to perform with a young
audience.

Effect

A 'mind-reading' trick in which a volunteer chooses
one of three picture cards. The performer correctly
predicts which card is chosen.

Equipment

A medium-sized envelope, a smaller envelope, and a
card to fit inside this envelope. Three sheets of white
card, each 15 x 10 cm (6 x 4 in). A marker pen and an
ordinary pen.

Preparation

Use the marker pen to draw a picture on each of the
three cards. On one card draw a house, on the second
draw a car, and on the third draw a bicycle (**1**).

1

Now carefully set up your prediction envelope. On the small card write with an ordinary pen, 'I knew you would pick the house!' Put the card inside the smaller envelope, seal the envelope, and on its front write, 'I knew you would pick the car!' Put this envelope inside the larger one and on the front of this write, 'I knew you would pick the bicycle!' Check that you have set up the prediction envelope correctly (**2**).

2

Now, whichever card a spectator chooses you can correctly predict the card by showing the appropriate message which you have set up beforehand. You need to be careful, of course, only to show the right message, and not one of the others. Start the trick with the envelope face down so that the message on the front is not visible.

Performing

● At the start of the trick openly place your prediction envelope down on one side, saying, 'This is my prediction as to what will happen.'

● Hand the three picture cards to one of the audience. Ask her to shuffle them and then get her to choose one. Add, 'Are you sure you want to choose that one?', so allowing her the opportunity to change her mind if she wants to.

● Continue, 'Well, that is strange, because that is the card I predicted.' Reach for the prediction envelope and display the message which matches her choice. For example, if she chooses the bicycle, simply turn over the envelope and show your message. Is she chooses the car, open the large envelope and take out the smaller one and turn it to face the audience. If she chooses the house, open the smaller envelope without showing its face to the audience, and then take out the card inside and show this to the audience. Whatever the choice, you can match it with the right message.

● Quickly move on to the next trick before your audience has time to figure out how the trick is done. Ask for your cards back and dispose of the envelopes carefully, so the audience does not see them.

● COLOUR MYSTERY

A highly effective trick to use with a young audience.

Effect

The performer is able to determine correctly the colour of a crayon placed in a tube behind her back.

Equipment

Six wax crayons of the same length and shape but of different colours. An opaque plastic tube with a stopper at one or both ends and which is big enough to hold a crayon (an old-fashioned cigar tube or similar is suitable) (**1**).

1

Preparation

Practise the trick thoroughly so that you can unseal the tube behind your back while carrying on a conversation with the audience. Also practise acting out your 'second sight' as convincingly as possible.

Performing

● Hand the six crayons to a member of the audience and, turning your back to him, ask him to choose one crayon and put it in the plastic tube and seal the top.

● Still with your hands behind your back, get him to place the tube in your hands and ask him to put the rest of the crayons in his pocket or hide them somewhere else.

● Now turn to face the audience and tell them what has happened so far. Meanwhile, with your hands behind your back (away from the audience's view), unseal the tube and tip it gently to allow the crayon to emerge slightly from one end. Scrape a finger or thumb nail against the crayon (**2**) and then reseal the tube with the crayon inside. All this is happening while you are talking to the audience.

2

● Continue, 'I will now try and use my second sight to see which colour crayon is inside the tube.' Saying this, bring the tube slowly up to your forehead. As you do so, glance at your finger or thumb nail and note the scraped off wax beneath it. You now know the colour of the crayon inside the tube.

● Close your eyes and take your time using your 'second sight' to 'see' the colour of the crayon inside the tube. The more effective your acting, the more dramatic the presentation of the trick.

● Finally, state the colour, and finish by opening the tube and taking out the crayon to confirm that you are right.

◆ NEWSPAPER PREDICTION

A trick best performed on an audience of older children.

Effect

The performer predicts precisely where a spectator will tell him to cut a newspaper column.

✚ Equipment

A newspaper, a pair of scissors and glue or clear adhesive tape. An envelope, paper and pencil.

Preparation

Carefully cut a column from the newspaper, choosing one where the headline is large. Cut off the headline (**1**), turn the column of text upside down, and then neatly stick or tape the headline to the now upside down column. Do this so that the join is not visible.

1

Now trim the bottom end of the column so that the cut end is close to the text (**2**).

2

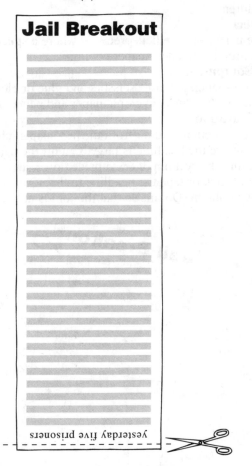

On the slip of paper write out the line of type furthest from the headline. This is your 'prediction'. Put it in a sealed envelope.

Performing

● Give the sealed envelope to a member of the audience.

● Hold up the column so the audience can see the headline (but they should not be so close that they can see the column text is upside down).

● Read out some text from about one-third of the way down the column. If you cannot read upside down easily, memorize a line or two. Remember, you are trying to give the appearance that the newspaper column is the right way up.

● Now take the scissors in your other hand, saying to a member of the audience, 'I will run the scissors up and down the column. Say "Stop" and I will cut the column at that point. OK?'

● Go ahead and follow the spectator's instructions, making the cut at the chosen place (**3**). Cut carefully so

3

the break is exactly horizontal and between one line of text and the next. The cut-off end of the column will now flutter to the ground.

● Get a member of the audience to read out the top line of the cut-off column.

● Now ask the spectator holding the sealed envelope to open it and read out the message – it will match the line read out.

● Discard your headline and text in a safe place, away from prying eyes.

◆ **BOOK TEST**

Another trick best performed on an audience of older children.

Effect

The performer hands a book to a member of the audience and then enlists the help of three people in choosing a random number between 1 and 99. This number determines which page is chosen from the book. The performer then 'mind-reads' the first word on that page.

Equipment

A book containing at least 100 pages, 78 rectangles of card, each 12.5 x 7.5 cm (5 x 3 in), a marker pen, a pencil and a rubber band.

Preparation

Prepare a pack of alphabet (lexicon) cards as follows. For each letter of the alphabet prepare three cards. For each card use the marker pen and simply write the appropriate capital letter in the centre of the card (**1**). Now take one of the cards for letter Q (this letter rarely comes up more than once in a word). With a pencil

1   **2**

write on this all the page numbers from 1–99. Next to each number write the first word found on that page of the book you are using (**2**). Assemble the cards in alphabetical order. The Q card with the information you want will therefore be in the centre of the pack. Enclose the cards in a rubber band and place them in your pocket. You are ready to perform the demonstration of your powers.

Performing

● Give the book to a member of the audience and ask her to flick through it to check that it is just a normal book – each page is different.

● Now explain that you are going to ask for help in choosing a random number between 1 and 99.

● Ask one person to call out a number from 1 to 9, ask another to call out another number from 1 to 9, and then ask a third to decide which of these two numbers (if they are different) should go first. The resulting two-digit number determines which page is to be selected.

● Ask the person with the book to turn to that page number and look at the first word on the page. Ask him to concentrate hard on that word.

● Explain that you are going to try and find that word by using telepathy – thought transference. Take out the cards from your pocket and explain that you are going to use these cards to spell out the word. Turn the cards to face the audience and riffle through the cards to show that they are simply cards with letters on (the pencil marks on the special Q card will not show up if you riffle through the pack quickly).

● Ask everyone to be quiet and still and say that you are going to try and 'read' the sender's mind.

● Start sorting through the cards, and take out the vowels – A,E,I,O,U – and lay them on the table (**3**). As you do this, secretly hunt for the special Q card and when you have located it, find the word which appears at the beginning of the chosen page.

3

● Ask the 'sender' to concentrate hard. Meanwhile, close your eyes as if deep in thought. Slowly, open them and then take the cards for the vowels in the chosen word. For example, if the word is BEAR take an E and an A and place them in front of you (**4**).

● Still concentrating, hunt for the remaining letters, but seem to make a mistake or two along the way, which you later correct. This misleads the audience into thinking that you really are 'mind-reading'. In our

4

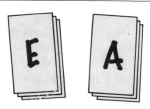

example, you might hunt for the letter B and then, to confuse the audience, search for the letter T, to make the word BEAT. Concentrate hard, change your mind, and correct the word to BEAR.

5

● Pretend that this demonstration has been a real effort of will. Thank the 'sender' for his help, pocket the cards, and then take a bow.

◆ MYSTERIOUS MAGAZINES

A more subtle variation on the Book Test (see p. 166).

Effect

The performer asks a volunteer to choose one of six magazines. He then enlists the help of four other people in choosing a particular word on a particular line of a particular page of the magazine. The volunteer finds this word and concentrates on it. The performer then proceeds to 'read her mind' and correctly writes down the chosen word on a piece of paper.

Equipment

Six different magazines (Sunday newspaper colour supplements are best), plus a further three magazines which are exact duplicates of three of them. Staple extractor and a stapler. Paper and pencil.

Preparation

With the aid of a staple extractor carefully remove the covers from the three duplicate magazines (**1b**, **2b**, **3b**). In the same way, remove the covers of magazines (**4**, **5**, **6**) and use these covers to form the outside of the duplicates. Replace the removed staples with new ones carefully positioned in the same holes. Done properly, the three doctored duplicates should appear not to have been tampered with. You now have six magazines, the covers being all different, but the interiors of three of them are identical with the other three. Pair them off in your mind so that you know which covers contain matching interiors.

Performing

● Show the magazines to the audience and, without actually saying so, indicate that they are all different.

● Get a volunteer to pick one of the magazines. Stress that her choice is not influenced by you in any way. She can, in fact, change her mind at this point, if she wishes.

● Once she has made the choice, put the remaining five magazines to one side.

● Now ask the volunteer to turn to the back of her magazine and say how many pages it contains, say 50.

● Get a second person to choose a number between 1 and 50, say 26. This will be the chosen page which the volunteer should then turn to.

● Ask the volunteer to say how many columns of print are on this page. A third person then chooses one of the columns, say the second, and says this out loud.

● Get a fourth person to give a number which represents the line in this column. The volunteer finds this line, say line 21, and then says how many words are on it. A fifth person then chooses one of the words, say the fourth, and the volunteer finds it.

● At this point, casually pick up one of the discarded magazines, making sure it is the duplicate of the volunteer's magazine. Pretend to run through the process carried out so far, using your own magazine to show the steps (but do not show the contents of the magazine to the audience). For example, 'You've chosen page 26, the 2nd column, the 21st line and the 4th word.' As you do this, you turn and count to the right place, and you find, of course, the chosen word – but don't say anything. Check with the volunteer, 'Is that right?'

● You now discard your magazine, pick up the pencil, pass it to the volunteer and ask her to circle the chosen word.

● Take back the pencil, and ask the volunteer to concentrate hard on the chosen word. Meanwhile, close your eyes and appear to be concentrating too.

● After a few seconds, take a paper and pencil and start to write out the chosen word. Make sure you make one or two errors, for example, writing LOFT, and then LIFT. Then ask the volunteer to concentrate harder and close your eyes once more before crossing out your earlier tries and writing LIGHT – the correct word (**2**).

2

◆ IT'S ALL DONE WITH THE HANDS

A very convincing demonstration of 'psychometric' powers – the ability to match an object to its owner.

Effect

Five members of the audience are asked to sign their names on a slip of paper. Each person puts their signed paper in an envelope which is then sealed. The envelopes are collected by one of the spectators. The performer takes the envelopes and then correctly 'divines' which envelope belongs to which person.

Equipment

Five envelopes (enclosed by a paper band), five sheets of paper 7.5 x 5 cm (3 x 2 in) and five pencils. Also a blunt cutlery knife.

Preparation

The 'trick' relies on an ingenious method for marking the envelopes. Lay an envelope on the table and then firmly press on a knife blade, running it along the edge next to the flap (**1**). This becomes envelope (**a**).

1

Repeat the procedure with the next envelope, but
running the blade along the left edge with the flap
uppermost. This envelope is (**b**). Envelopes (**c**) and (**d**)
are treated in a similar fashion, but pressing the right-
hand and bottom edges of the envelope respectively (**2**).
The fifth envelope (**e**) is untreated.

2

Envelope a

Envelope b   Envelope c

Envelope d

All the envelopes are now distinguishable by touch.
Envelopes (**a**), (**b**), (**c**) and (**d**) have one edge which is
flattened. It is then simply a case of remembering, and
then detecting, which envelope has which side
flattened. Envelope (**e**) has no flattened sides.
Pack the envelopes into a paper band in the right order
from (**a**) to (**e**), with (**a**) uppermost (**3**).

3

Performing
● Show the five slips of paper to the audience. Hand them to a volunteer and ask him to check them. While he is doing this, hand a pencil to five other members of audience.
● Ask the volunteer to give a slip of paper to each person who has a pencil.
● Now get the five people to sign their slip of paper. While they are doing this, remove the paper band from around the envelopes and then go round and hand an envelope to each of the five (mentally noting the order in which you have given out the envelopes).
● Get each person to put their slip of paper inside the envelope and then seal it.
● Ask the volunteer to collect the envelopes, and shuffle them.
● Take the envelopes, place them on the table in front of you, and then take one and carefully hold it between your fingers so that you are holding all four sides of the envelope with the flap uppermost (**4**).

4

● With your eyes closed, concentrate as though you are trying to sense which person's signature is inside. You should be able to tell which envelope it is by noting which side, if any, has a sharp edge.

● Open your eyes and then give the envelope to the appropriate person, but ask him or her not to open it.

● Continue in this way, taking your time, and apparently 'divining' which envelope (and enclosed signature) belongs to which person.

● When you have handed out all the envelopes, ask the five people to open them. Inside, each will find the piece of paper with their signature.

✖ TIPPING THE BALANCE

This demonstration of mind over matter is aimed at an adult audience. It works best in a warm, dry room.

Effect

The performer balances two matches on the edge of a matchbox. He then gets a spectator to choose one of two matches. By exercising the power of the mind, the magician can make the match topple and fall.

✚ Equipment

Two unused wooden matches, a small matchbox and a glass of water (or, better still, vodka).

Preparation

Secretly dip about 1 cm ($^1/_2$ in) of the non-striking end of the match into the glass of water (or vodka) for 30–40 seconds. Then take the match out and wipe off the surface liquid with your fingers.

Performing

● Start the trick with the two matchsticks lying side by side across the top of the matchbox (**1**). You need to

1

know which is the 'dipped' matchstick.

● Now ask a spectator to pick one match for her and one match for you. In reality you make the choice. If she points to the non-dipped match say, 'Alright, you have that one and I'll have the other.' If she points to the dipped match say, 'OK, so that's the one I'll use. Now while I concentrate on it I want you to concentrate on the other one.'

● Now move the matches over slightly, one at a time, so that they are delicately balanced on one edge of the matchbox. This is best done by gently nudging the tail end of the match with one hand while using the other hand to stop the match overbalancing (**2**) (see over). If the match overbalances, gently nudge it the other way. When you have finished, both matches should be parallel and with their heads tilted down by the same degree (**3**).

● Continue, 'Right. Concentrate on your match and I'll concentrate on mine.' Alternatively, you can both concentrate on the same match (the dipped one) and get the rest of the audience to concentrate on the other one.

2

3   **4**

Whatever you decide, in time the liquid will evaporate from the dipped match and slowly but surely the match will tip further and then fall (**4**). If you set the trick up properly, you can convince the audience that it is your concentration that has made the match fall. A true case of 'mind over matter'.

◆ THE PENDULUM WILL FIND YOU OUT

You will need to practise this one to convince yourself
that it really does work!

Effect

The performer is able to find out what a person is
thinking simply by getting that person to hold a
pendulum.

Equipment

A white cotton thread about 40 cm (16 in) long. A
finger ring. Three white cards 12.5 x 10 cm (5 x 4 in).
A pen.

Preparation

Tie the ring neatly to the end of the thread (**1**). Practise
the trick several times with friends or relatives to
convince yourself that it actually does work.

Performing

● Hand the three cards and the pen to a member of the
audience. Turn your back and ask him to sign his name
on one of the cards.

● Still with your back turned, get him to lay the three
cards in front of him in a row, with the signature on the
marked card face down. He decides where the marked
card is positioned.

● Now turn back and face the spectator. Explain that
you do not know which card he signed, nor where he

has placed the card. Continue by saying, 'But you are going to help me find the card, believe it or not.'

● Continue, 'I'm going to ask you three questions shortly to which your answer will be yes or no. Don't tell me the answer – the pendulum will speak for you. If the truthful answer to my question is yes, the pendulum will swing backwards and forwards in a straight line. If the truthful answer is no, the pendulum will swing around in a small circle. Have you got that? Just nod if the answer is yes.'

● Now show him how you want him to hold the pendulum, absolutely still to start with, between his thumb and first finger (**2**).

2

● Now run through everything once again: 'If the truthful answer is yes the pendulum will swing to and fro; if no, it will swing in a circle. Right. Here are the three questions.'

● Point to one of the cards and ask, 'Is this the signed card? Concentrate. Think yes or no.' Now watch what the pendulum does. If it swings back and forth you have found the card first time (3). If not, move on to another card, and repeat the question, while pointing at the next card. The pendulum needs to be stationary before each 'reading' is taken.

3   **Yes**   **No**

● As the performer, you can choose to stop as soon as you find the card for which the answer is yes. Or you can continue until you have checked all three cards and confirmed that one is yes and the other two are no. When you are ready, turn over the card which is the marked one.

Note: This trick really does seem to be mysterious! According to psychologists, the pendulum signal works by a combination of suggestion and response. You have suggested to the spectator that the truthful answer yes will produce a back and forth movement of the pendulum, while a truthful no response will produce a circular movement. His unconscious mind is triggered by your questions to produce minute, imperceptible movements in the pendulum-holding hand so generating the required pendulum movement. Such a reaction is called a psychomotor response, and, believe it or not, the trick works well with most people most of the time.

◆ **TAP IT OUT**
A trick best done in your own home. You need a good memory and your volunteer needs to be able to spell.
Effect
The performer arranges seven objects on the table. He asks a spectator to think of one of them. The performer then taps each of them in turn with a wand. For each tap, the spectator has to mentally spell out one letter of the name of the object she has in mind. On the last letter spelt she should stop. Amazingly, the performer's wand will be on the same object thought of by the spectator.
Equipment
A cup, a bowl, a glass, a saucer, an ashtray, a matchbox, a corkscrew. A pencil and paper. A wand (or a pencil).
Preparation
Commit the seven items and their corresponding numbers to memory:

1. Cup   5. Ashtray
2. Bowl   6. Matchbox
3. Glass   7. Corkscrew
4. Saucer

Arrange the objects on the table before the trick starts.
Do not put them in sequence, but it helps if you arrange
them in a similar pattern each time you do the trick (**1**).
This helps you remember where they are and means
that you have one less thing to worry about.

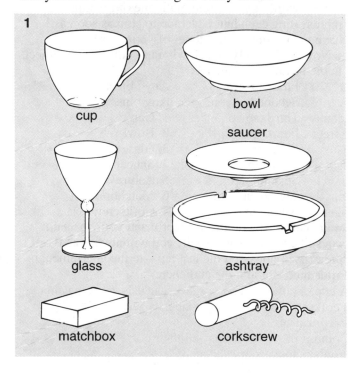

1

cup

bowl

saucer

glass

ashtray

matchbox

corkscrew

Performing
● Point out each object you have on the table and as you do so, give its name. Do this in a random order.
● Now ask a spectator to think of one of the objects.
● Explain what you want her to do. 'I will tap an object, and as I do so I want you to mentally spell out one letter of the name of the object. For example, if you think of cup and I tap the glass first, think of C for cup, on the second tap, the letter U, and so on. Simply spell out the word in your mind, with one of my taps representing each letter. Get me to stop as soon as I have tapped out the last letter of your word.'
● Now deliberately and slowly tap out the seven objects in the following sequence:

First tap	-	Any object
Second tap	-	Any object
Third tap	-	1. Cup
Fourth tap	-	2. Bowl
Fifth tap	-	3. Glass
Sixth tap	-	4. Saucer
Seventh tap	-	5. Ashtray
Eighth tap	-	6. Matchbox
Ninth tap	-	7. Corkscrew

● Providing you do this correctly and your spectator doesn't cheat (or can't spell) you will always arrive at the chosen object on the last tap – to the amazement of your spectator and the audience.

6. Mathematical magic

Mathematical discoveries provide a rich harvest for performers who choose to exploit the magical properties of numbers. Most of these tricks come under the category 'self-working'. Simply follow the instructions and the tricks work by themselves, without any sleight of hand or other deception. In many cases, you can use a mentalist approach to describe your magic feat. As with other performances of mental magic, much depends on your ability to convey a sense of mystery and wonder. Use the word 'test', 'demonstration' or 'experiment' rather than 'trick' to describe what you are doing. Again, this reinforces the idea that you are using mental powers, not a conjuring trick, to achieve the special effect.

● I'VE GOT YOUR NUMBER
This quick and easy trick works every time, providing your volunteer can carry out your instructions and can do simple arithmetic. You, the performer, have little to do.
Effect
The performer writes a prediction on a slip of paper. He then asks a volunteer to think of a number, and then gets her to perform some simple arithmetic with the number. At no stage is the performer given any indication of what the original number is. The volunteer completes the arithmetic and the number with which she is left matches that predicted by the performer.

Equipment
Two pieces of paper and a pencil.

Preparation
No special preparation is required. You will, of course, need to memorize all the instructions.

Performing
● At the start of the trick write this prediction on a piece of paper, taking care not to show the writing to any member of the audience: 'You will finish with the number 1089.'

● Ask a volunteer to call out any three-digit number in which all the digits are different; for example, 257.

● Give the volunteer a pencil and paper and ask her to write this number in reverse; in this example, she would write 752.

● Now get her to subtract the first three-digit number from the second, or vice versa, subtracting the smaller number from the larger. In this case, the calculation would be:

$$\begin{array}{r} 752 \\ - 257 \\ \hline 495 \end{array}$$

● Now ask the volunteer to reverse this total, and add the two three-digit numbers together:

$$\begin{array}{r} 495 \\ + 594 \\ \hline 1089 \end{array}$$

● Sometimes she will end up with 99, a two-digit number:

$$\begin{array}{r} 483 \\ - 384 \\ \hline 99 \end{array}$$

● In this case, ask the volunteer to add 99 to 99 to get a three-digit number:

$$\begin{array}{r} 99 \\ + 99 \\ \hline 198 \end{array}$$

● Now ask the volunteer to reverse the total, and add the two three-digit numbers together:

$$\begin{array}{r} 198 \\ + 891 \\ \hline 1089 \end{array}$$

● Get someone else to open your piece of paper, which has been in full view throughout, and read out what is written upon it. Your prediction proves to be correct! Note: Try this trick several times. Whatever three-digit number you choose, when you follow the instructions correctly, you always finish up with 1089.

◆ **THINK OF A NUMBER**
A variation on the previous trick. It requires the performer to do a small amount of mental arithmetic.
Effect
The performer asks a volunteer to choose a two-digit number and gets him to tell her and the audience what this is. The performer then asks the volunteer to perform a series of simple calculations which involve the volunteer's own personal details (and which the performer cannot be expected to know) plus other information provided by the audience. At an early stage, the performer writes a prediction on a slip of paper. Later, when this prediction is compared with the volunteer's answer, they are found to match.

Equipment

Two pieces of paper and two pencils.

Preparation

No special preparation is required other than memorizing the instructions and practising some simple mental arithmetic.

Performing

● Ask a volunteer to think of a two-digit number and get him to tell you and the audience what this number is; for example, 65.

● Get the volunteer to write this number on a piece of paper, explaining that you want him to do some simple arithmetic. Say you will do the same (in fact, you write down another number – a prediction – that is easily calculated in your head once you have the volunteer's chosen number).

● Now ask the volunteer to write his year of birth underneath the number but keep this to himself. For example:

65 (*volunteer's chosen number*)
1979 (*year of birth*)

● Ask someone else to call out a famous event and the year that it happened; say, 1066 and the Battle of Hastings. The volunteer should add this to his list.

● Finally, ask a volunteer to write down how old he will be at the end of the year and how many years it has been since the event called out by the spectator. He may need to do a separate calculation to work this out.

● Now run through again what you've asked him to do, emphasizing those items you did not know when you wrote on your paper, and those items which even now you do not know.

● Now get the volunteer to add up his list of numbers and tell you what the final total is. His calculations, taking the current year as 1996, should look like this:

$$65 \ (\textit{volunteer's chosen number})$$
$$1979 \ (\textit{year of birth})$$
$$1066 \ (\textit{year of Battle of Hastings})$$
$$17 \ (\textit{volunteer's age at end of year})$$
$$\underline{930} \ (\textit{years since Battle of Hastings})$$
$$\text{Total} = 4057$$

● Ask someone else to unfold the piece of paper on which you've written a number. Your prediction – and the volunteer's answer – are the same!

● What is the secret? All you have to do is carry in your head twice the number of the year in which you are performing. In 1996, for example, this number is 3992 i.e. 2 x 1996. When the volunteer's two-digit number is mentioned, you add his number to 3992 and write this answer on a piece of paper which is disclosed at the end. Thus, if the volunteer's number was 65, the final answer (in 1996) will be 3992 + 65 = 4057 (the same answer as that calculated by the volunteer).

◆ MAGIC SQUARE

The effect of this trick on your audience has to be seen to be believed. You will go up in their estimation!

Effect

The performer asks a member of the audience for a number between 50 and 100. The performer then draws a square on a piece of paper and divides this into 16 smaller squares. He rapidly fills the squares with numbers in an apparently random manner. The large square, now filled with numbers, is passed to the spectator. The spectator discovers her chosen number is the sum of each vertical line of numbers, each horizontal line, the two diagonals, and the central block and corner blocks of four squares.

Equipment

Paper, pencil and a ruler.

Preparation

You will need to memorize the method for constructing the square of numbers and the positions of numbers 1–12. Once this is achieved, practise using different guessed numbers to develop your ability to enter numbers quickly. About 10 minutes' practice a day over a fortnight will make you an expert!

Performing

● In full view of your audience use pencil and ruler to draw a square on the piece of paper. Then divide the square into 16 smaller squares (**1**).

● Ask a spectator for any number between 50 and 100.

● Now write the numbers 1–9 in the squares as shown

1

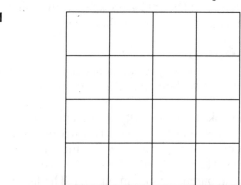

(2). (It is probably best for you to devise your own strategy for remembering where these numbers go. One way of checking is to ensure that each vertical group of numbers adds up to nine, with the number 9 on its own in the bottom right-hand corner. The number 6 – an upside-down 9 – is next to the 9.)

● Now add the numbers 10, 11 and 12 in the positions shown (3).

2

	1		7
	8		2
5		3	
4		6	9

3

	1	12	7
11	8		2
5	10	3	
4		6	9

● You are now left with four spaces to fill. Subtract 20 from the spectator's chosen number – for example, if the number is 66, subtract 20, giving 46. Call this number **N** and enter this number in the first square of the first line (**4**).

4

Enter N	1	12	7
11	8	Enter N-1	2
5	10	3	Enter N+2
4	Enter N+1	6	9

● Move to the second line and enter the number **N - 1**, in other words 46 – 1 = 45, in the empty square.
● Move to the third line and enter the number **N + 2**, in other words 46 + 2 = 48, in the empty square.
● Finally, in the fourth line, enter **N + 1** as the missing number.
● The magic square is now complete (**5**). Hand it to your spectator. She – and the audience – will be amazed at how the different combinations of four numbers –

verticals, horizontals, diagonals and blocks – will add up to her chosen number, 66.

5

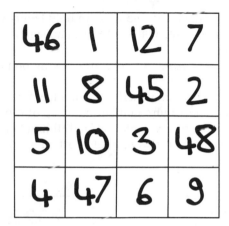

46	1	12	7
11	8	45	2
5	10	3	48
4	47	6	9

◆ THE NINES HAVE IT

Superficially similar to the Book Test (see p. 166) and Mysterious Magazines (see p. 169), this trick works on a very different principle and is foolproof.

Effect

The performer hands a magazine to a spectator. She then asks another person to think of a four-figure number made up of four different digits. The performer does not know this number, but simply asks the spectator to perform a series of calculations on it until he is left with a single-figure number. The performer knows what this is, and directs the other spectator to turn to that page of the magazine – the performer has predicted that page and a message is waiting there!

Equipment
A magazine, a marker pen, a paper and pencil.
Preparation
On page 9 of the magazine write in bold letters with the marker pen GOT THERE BEFORE YOU! and sign it.
Performing
● Hand the magazine to a spectator, asking him not to open it.
● Hand the paper and pencil to a volunteer and get him to think of a four-figure number made up of four different digits; for example, 7923. Tell him not to disclose his number to you, but to write it down on a piece of paper (**1**).

1

7923

2

7923
2937

● Now get the volunteer to jumble up the four digits of the number and write these down below the first number (**2**).
● Get him to subtract the smaller number from the larger one (**3**).

3

7923
−2937
———
4986

• He should then take this total and add the digits together (**4**). If he is left with two digits he should add these together until he is left with one digit (**5**).

4

7923
−2937
———
4986

4+9+8+6=27

5

7923
−2937
———
4986

4+9+8+6=27

2+7=9

• Continue 'I know the number you've got. I got there before you.' And saying this, ask the volunteer to get the spectator with the magazine to turn to that page. There, the audience will find your message and be suitably surprised.

Note: When the instructions for this trick are followed, the final number is always a 9. Interestingly, the two-digit number obtained beforehand, if there is one, will also be a multiple of 9.

◆ MAGIC STAR

This trick employing the magic star can be repeated, to great effect, particularly with a young audience.

Effect

The performer gets a volunteer to throw two dice – the numbers obtained are kept secret from the performer. The volunteer then makes some simple mental calculations based on features of the magic star and the final total is written in the centre of the star. From this total the performer correctly determines the two numbers shown by the dice.

Equipment

A marker pen and a metric ruler. A white card 15 x 10 cm (6 x 4 in). Two dice of different colours (for example, one white, the other black). A duster or a similar-sized piece of material. A pencil and paper.

Preparation

With the ruler and marker pen, carefully draw a five-pointed star of the dimensions shown (**1**).

You will need to memorize the directions to give to the spectator, but they are quite straightforward.

Performing

● Ask a spectator to throw one die, say the white, while your back is turned. Say he throws a 3. Ask him to note the number thrown but to keep the number from you. Get him to then cover the die with the duster. Give him the paper and pencil in case he wants to use them in the calculations which follow.

1

● Now bring out the magic star and explain that you will use it to help unravel the mystery of this trick. Point to the two horns (the downward-pointing arms of the star) and explain that these are significant. In a black magic star they point upwards, representing the horns of the devil, but in friendly or white magic, the horns point downwards.

● Continue advising the spectator, 'The number 2 is important, so take the number you threw and multiply it by 2.' In the example here, this would give 3 x 2 = 6.

● Now add, 'The star has five points – this is significant – so add 5 to the number you have.' This would give 6 + 5 = 11.

● 'The star also has five angles between the points –
also significant – so, please multiply your last total by
5.' This would give 11 x 5 = 55.
● 'Now take the other die – the black one – and throw
that. Add this number to your last number.' If the 6 is
thrown, this would give 55 + 6 = 61.
● Continue with, 'Now cover both dice with the duster
so I can't see them.'
● And finish with, 'Now write your final total in the
centre of the star.'
● When this is done, a glance at the number and some
simple mental arithmetic enables you to work out not
only the values shown by the dice – but which die
shows which number. How? Simply subtract 25 from
the final number. That will give you the numbers shown
on the two dice. For example, 61 – 25 = 36 showing
that a 3 was thrown for the first die – the white one –
and a 6 for the second die – the black one.
Note: This trick works every time, and the magic star
can be used again and again if the centre number is
rubbed out each time. But don't repeat the trick more
than once in a single performance, or the audience will
catch on how it is done.

◆ **BEAT THE CALCULATOR**
The performer beats two challengers hands down.
Effect
The performer challenges two spectators to a
mathematical contest – the performer pitting his mental
arithmetic against the calculators of the spectators.
Performer and spectators perform the same calculation,
but the performer gets there before them.

Equipment
Three sheets of paper and three pencils. Two simple electronic calculators.

Preparation
Practise the trick several times, using different numbers, to convince yourself that it works each and every time.

Performing

● Start the trick by explaining that, in an age of high technology, there are still some calculations better done by the human brain, rather than a computer or calculator.

● Find two people from the audience who wish to take part in a simple mathematical challenge. Call one challenger A and the other challenger B.

● Give A and B a paper and pencil and get them to write the letters A and B separated by a couple of centimetres (about an inch) (**1**). You do the same.

1

● Ask person A to provide a three-figure number composed of different digits; for example, 625. All three of you then write this number down under letters A and B (**2**).

2

● Now get person B to think of a three-figure number made up of three different digits, say 784. You all put this number under 625 in column A (**3**).

3

● Explain that you don't want to be left out of the proceedings, and you'd like to throw in a three-figure number too. To the others, this number will appear random. In reality, you have decided on the number by mentally subtracting B's number, in this case 784, from your personal magic number, 999. This gives 999 − 784 = 215, and it is 215 which you and the others write in column B (**4**). Now for the challenge.

4

● Give A and B each a calculator. Explain you want
them to multiply together the two numbers in their own
column, and then get together with the other person and
add their totals together. They have the calculators, you
will do it in your head.

● Once they are clear what they have to do, say 'Ready
steady, go' and start. You will be able to do the
calculation very quickly and here is the method.
Subtract 1 from the first number, in this case giving
624, and write this down. Then subtract this number
from the magic number 999, giving 999 − 624 = 375,
and then write this down. The six-figure number,
624,375 is the right answer. It has taken you seconds.
Meanwhile, the two challengers will still be working on
their calculations (**5**) (see over). They should get the
same answer as you, but you will have beaten them
hands down.

● Don't repeat the trick with the same audience.

5

Note: The magic formula for the performer to remember is:

● Your number – to be put in column B – is the difference between the second (challenger B's) number and 999.

● To get the final total subtract 1 from the first number (challenger A's) and write this number down. This gives you the first three digits. Then subtract this three-digit number from 999. This gives you the second three digits.

7. Miscellaneous magic

This chapter contains a potpourri of tricks and novelties which use a variety of props. Some are more suitable for party tricks or stage magic, others for close-up performance.

● WAND VANISHES HANDKERCHIEF
Effect
A handkerchief appears to vanish, having been pushed into a simple cone of newspaper.
Equipment
A silk handkerchief, a sheet of newspaper and a specially designed, hollow wand with a steel rod inside, obtainable from a magic shop.

Preparation
Check that the steel rod is free to slide out from inside the special wand.
Performing
● Roll a sheet of newspaper into a cone (**1**, see over). Show the audience the open end of the cone and use the wand as a pointer to push down into the cone to demonstrate that it is empty.
● While doing this, slide the steel rod out from the wand and grip it through the bottom of the cone (**2**, see over).
● Once this is done it is important to keep the cone upright so the steel rod cannot be seen by the audience.

● Next, place a handkerchief over the mouth of the
cone (**3**). Tell the audience that you are going to make
the handkerchief disappear.

● Taking the wand, push the handkerchief down inside the cone (**4**). What you are really doing is placing the wand 'case' back over the steel rod and, in doing so, forcing the handkerchief up into the wand (**5**).

● Place the wand on the table and, taking one corner of the newspaper, shake out the newspaper to show that the handkerchief has vanished!

4

5

● BIG WAND FROM TINY PURSE

A trick in which the conjurer apparently produces a wand from a small purse into which it could not possibly fit.

Effect

The performer produces a small purse, opening it to show the audience that it is empty. The next moment he opens the purse and a 40 cm (15 in) wand is magically produced!

✛ Equipment

A small purse, a magician's wand, a rubber band and a pair of scissors.

Preparation

Cut a 4 cm (1½ in) hole in one end of the purse (**1**). Place the purse in your *right* pocket. Insert the wand into your *left* sleeve and secure it by placing a rubber band not too tightly around your wrist (**2**).

1

2

Performing

● Facing your audience, casually take the purse from your right pocket, using your right hand. Open it and show the audience that it is empty. Be careful to keep the hole in the purse hidden by having it next to your palm.

● Next, place the purse into your left hand with the hole nearest your wrist (**3**). Open the purse and pretend to feel about in it for the wand. As you do this, put your fingers through the hole and take hold of the wand that is still attached to your wrist.

● Slowly, pull the wand out of your sleeve, through the hole, and out of the purse (**4**). Show the wand to the audience so that they can check it is real. Meanwhile, return the purse to your pocket and begin the next trick.

3

4

◆ WHICH WAY?

A fast and funny trick with which to begin your
performance. Use the patter described here, or make up
your own story.

Effect

The performer tells a story about a journey and uses a
card with arrows to describe her progress. It starts off
clearly enough, but as she continues, the arrows seem
to miraculously change direction, much to the
amazement and confusion of the audience.

Equipment

A 25 x 25 cm (10 x 10 in) square of card. A marker pen
and a ruler.

Preparation

Carefully draw an arrow on each side of the card (**1**). It
is important that the arrows are at right angles to each
other, exactly as shown.

Practise the trick, along with your accompanying patter,
so that your performance is fast and funny.

1

Front of card   **Back of card**

Performing

● Start the trick with the arrow on the back facing upwards and with the front arrow (on the side towards the audience) pointing from your right hand to your left hand (**2**). Hold the card at the top left and bottom right.

2

Left hand

Right hand

● Explain that on your journey here it was plain sailing for the first few miles. As you say this, turn the card over several times, pivoting it about your hands. As you do this, the arrow will always point from your right hand to your left.

● Continue, 'But as I came nearer things got a bit more complicated. I asked someone the way, but I think they misdirected me. For the next few miles I seemed to be turning right, then left, then right, zigzagging my way here. It was really confusing!' Saying this, shift your hands so that they are now holding the bottom left and top right of the card. Turn the card over several times. Now the arrow will shift direction, first one way, and then the other (**3**).

3

Right hand

Left hand

• Stop turning when the arrow is pointing from your left hand to your right.
• Continue with, 'Then I asked someone else, just to check I was on the right track. She didn't have a clue. I ended up going back the way I'd come.' Saying this, move you hands so that they are holding the bottom right and top left again. Rotate the card as you talk, and the arrow will point from your left hand to your right (**4**).
• 'By this time I was really fed up. I checked on the map and saw that I really needed to be going north.' As you say this, turn the card over from top to bottom but keeping your hands in place on the card (**5**). Your right hand will now be at the top, your left hand at the bottom, and the front arrow (facing the audience) will now be pointing up.

4

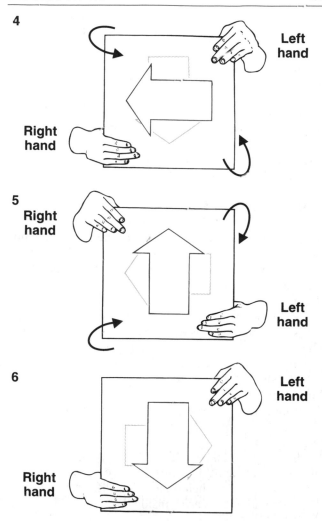

Left hand

Right hand

5
Right hand

Left hand

6

Left hand

Right hand

● When you now turn the card over several times, pivoting it between your hands, the arrow is always pointing upwards.

● 'But that still wasn't it! I still hadn't got here. I'd overshot, and had to double back a mile or so, travelling south.' And with that shift your right hand to the bottom and your left hand to the top. Turn over the card just once, and the arrow will be pointing down (**6**, see previous page).

● 'But as you see, I got here in the end.' And with that, toss the card aside and launch into your next trick.

●LOSING YOUR SHIRT

None of the other tricks in this book rely on a secret stooge or confederate – a member of the audience who is in league with you. This is the one trick that does. Make sure you choose a stooge who will keep quiet about the secret of the trick.

Effect

The performer goes to a male member of the audience and asks whether he has ever lost his shirt at gambling. When the answer is 'no' – the performer unbuttons the spectator's collar and cuffs and in one swift movement pulls the shirt off the spectator. A great party trick.

Equipment

The stooge needs to wear a shirt (preferably an old one) beneath a jacket or pullover.

Preparation

Get the stooge to take off his jacket or pullover and unbutton and take off his shirt. Lay the opened shirt across his back, and then button the cuffs around his wrists but without his arms inside the sleeves (**1**). Then

put the collar around his neck and button two or three
buttons at the front (two buttons if his shirt collar is
open; three buttons if he is going to wear a tie) (**2**).
Hold his jacket or pullover so he can get back into it

1

2

again. If he is wearing a tie, put that back on too. Make any final adjustments so that with his collar and cuffs visible, he looks as though he is wearing the shirt as normal.

Performing

● Look around the audience, as though you are searching for a likely candidate (in reality, of course, you have decided in advance who will be the other person in your trick).

● Go to your stooge and ask him, 'Have you ever lost your shirt at gambling?' When he answers, apparently unsuspectingly, 'No. Why?', reply with, 'Well, let me show you.'

● Proceed to unbutton his cuffs and then undo the two or three buttons at the front of the shirt (if he is wearing a tie undo that and remove it).

● Now count out loud, 'One, two, three', and with that grasp the back of his shirt collar and pull the shirt up hard and fast so that the shirt comes clear of the pullover or jacket.

● Finish with, 'And don't try that one at home folks!' and take a bow. Oh yes, don't forget to give your helper his shirt back!

● BALLOON CRAZY

A simple and effective balloon trick particularly suitable for a young boisterous audience.

Effect

The performer takes an inflated party balloon and proceeds to stick a hatpin straight into it. Amazingly, the balloon does not burst. With the balloon still

impaled on the pin, the performer invites someone else
to stick another pin in. This time, the balloon bursts.

✚ Equipment
Two or three large, patterned party balloons. Clear
adhesive tape and scissors. Two large, sharp hatpins.

Preparation
Inflate the balloon so that it is fairly taut and then knot
the neck of the balloon. Apply a square of clear
adhesive tape, about 2 x 2 cm (1 x 1 in), to one side of
the balloon (**1**).

1

Start the trick with the inflated balloon to hand, but
with the square of tape hidden from the audience's
view.

Prepare two or three balloons in advance, so that should
one burst before you do the trick you have another
ready on the table.

Performing
● Pick up the balloon and hand the two hatpins to a
spectator.

● Ask the spectator to check the pins and then hand one
back to you.

● Now continue, 'Of course, balloons and pins don't
mix very well. But this is a friendly balloon and if you
ask it nicely . . .' On saying this, hold the balloon
carefully in the crook of your left arm and proceed to
stick the hatpin into the balloon through the centre of
the square of adhesive tape (**2**). Keep the pin away from
the audience's direct view as you stick it into the
balloon.

● Turn the balloon sideways on so that the audience can
see the hatpin sticking out of the balloon (**3**).
● Now turn the balloon so that the hatpin is facing you
and away from the audience. Hold on to the hatpin so
that later, when the balloon bursts, it doesn't fly off and
hurt someone. Walk up to the spectator who is holding
the hatpin and ask her to stick the pin in, just as you
did.
● When she tries this, the balloon will burst. Finish
with, 'Ah. You didn't ask it nicely!' Take back the
spectator's hatpin and carefully dispose of the remains
of the balloon. Then get on with the next trick.

● STICKY FINGERS

A trick using a table knife. It works well with a young audience.

Effect

A knife appears to be stuck to the fingers. If anyone guesses the secret, the performer has another trick up his sleeve.

Equipment

A table knife, a pencil, and a wristwatch on your left wrist.

Preparation

Slip the pencil underneath your watchstrap and keep it hidden up your sleeve (**1**).

Performing

● Tell the audience, 'This trick is called sticky fingers. Watch!' Saying this, hold the knife upright in the clenched fist of your left hand (**2**, see over).

● Now bring your right hand over and clasp it around your left wrist. Slowly open the fingers of your left hand and, as you do so, extend the first finger of your right hand to press the knife against your left hand (**3**, see over). Seen from the front, the knife appears to be stuck to your fingers (**4**, see over).

● At this stage, it is possible that someone correctly guesses the secret of the trick. If not, then the trick is over and you are free to move on to the next trick. If they do guess correctly, you are ready to move on to the next stage of the trick.

● Run through the trick again, just as before, but this time use your right hand to pull out the pencil from your left sleeve. You can position your right hand exactly as before, but with the pencil between your forefinger and the knife (**5**).

● Now when you remove your right hand – as you will be told to do – press the knife against the pencil using your left hand. The knife will stay miraculously stuck to your fingers, dumbfounding the audience (**6**).

To complete the trick, pull the knife away from the pencil and toss it on the table. As the audience goes to examine the knife, push the pencil back up your sleeve. You can now show your empty hand to the audience as well.

◆ THE MAGIC KNIFE

Another trick which uses a knife. This one can be performed impromptu at the dinner table. It relies on a simple move and very few props.

Effect

The performer shows spectators a knife with four bits of tissue paper stuck to it – two on the front, two on the back. The papers are removed, and then magically reappear.

Equipment

A table knife. Four small squares of paper about 1 x 1 cm (½ x ½ in) torn from a paper napkin or tissue. A cup or glass of water.

Preparation

You will need to practise the 'paddle move' until you can do it smoothly and effortlessly. Just before performing the trick, wet each paper square in turn and stick it to the blade of the knife so that two squares are on one side and two on the other (**1**).

side a

side b

Performing
● Start with the knife held downwards between the thumb and first finger of your right hand (**2**).

● Explain that this knife looks like an ordinary one but, in fact, it is a magical one. Proceed to show the knife to the audience using a method of presentation called the 'paddle move'. This move gives the appearance that you are showing both sides of the knife when, in fact, you are showing only one side.
● The 'paddle move' is performed as follows: Turn the hand over and up, but as you do this, give the knife a half-turn by rotating it between your thumb and first finger (**3**, see over). On the way down, reverse the movements to bring the knife back to its original position.

3

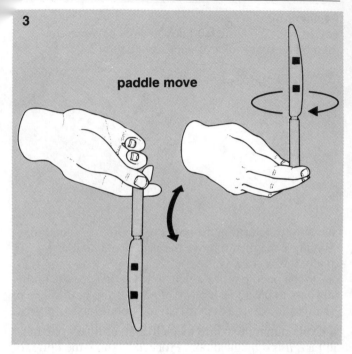

paddle move

- At this stage, show 'both sides' of the knife using the paddle move (in reality you are showing only one side of the knife).
- With the left hand, remove one piece of paper from the knife and pretend to throw it away, but actually keep it in your hand (**4**).
- Now do the paddle move, raising the knife to pretend to show the other side, but as you do so, return your left hand to the knife. It looks as though you are removing the paper from the other side of the knife. Really, you

are simply returning the paper to its original location. Having done this, remove the paper again but now really throw it away.

● Do the paddle move again. To the audience the knife appears to have lost a piece of paper from both sides; in reality it has lost a paper from only one side.

● Repeat the above moves to take away the second piece of paper on that side.

● Do the paddle move once more. To the audience the knife appears to be blank on both sides. In fact, it is blank on one side and has two papers on the other side.

● Click the fingers of your left hand and with a quick upward sweep of the right hand, revolve the knife in your fingers to bring the paper side to the front. The paper squares have magically returned! Do the paddle move once more to show the audience that the squares have returned to both sides.

● Carefully run your left thumb and first finger along the blade to remove the 'four' pieces of paper (really only two) and place them in your left pocket. You are left with a perfectly ordinary table knife to give the audience to inspect.

✖ UPSIDE DOWN MYSTERY
Make water defy gravity.
Effect
The performer shows the audience the classic trick of supporting water above a sheet of card. The trick is repeated and the card removed. Miraculously, the water is supported when the card is removed.
Equipment
A wine glass with mouth and foot of the same diameter (**1**). A disc of clear perspex of the same diameter as the foot of the glass. A piece of card 15 x 10 cm (6 x 4 in). A jug of water, a large plastic bowl and a towel.
Preparation
Wet the perspex disc and it will stick to the underside of the wine glass (**2**). The disc is now ready for use when needed.
Make sure the jug of water, the bowl, the towel and the card are all close at hand.

1   **2**

Performing

● Explain to the audience that you will demonstrate the classic trick where you can make water defy gravity, adding, 'I'm sure many of you know the trick.'

● Hold the wine glass upright in your right hand and over the bowl. Then carefully pour in water from the jug until the glass is absolutely full.

● With your left hand, place the sheet of card on top of the wine glass. Any water that might spill will fall into the bowl.

● With your left hand in place supporting the card, carefully turn over the glass (**3**).

● Take your hand away from under the card. The water is held in place by the card with no other support.

● Continue with, 'The problem is, when you take the card away, the water falls' and, saying this, slide the card off the mouth of the glass. Of course, the water will cascade into the bowl (**4**).

3

4

● Add, 'But there is an incantation I learned recently from an Oriental magician. Let's see how it works.'

● Fill the glass as before but this time, just before you place the card on top of the glass, sit the glass on your left hand (**5**).

● Bring your left hand up from below the glass, taking with it the perspex disc that has been concealed under the glass. Place your hand over the glass and as you do so, place the perspex disc snuggly over the mouth of the glass (**6**).

5   **6**

● Keep your hand over the glass, close your eyes and appear to concentrate hard while saying a secret magical incantation which no one can hear. Then remove your hand and place the card over the glass as before. Water may spill into the bowl.

● Holding the card in place with your left hand, turn the glass upside down as before. This time, however, when you slide the card across, the water will not fall into the bowl but will stay in the glass as if by magic (**7**).

● Allow the glass to stay like this for a few seconds, and then put your left hand over the mouth again, and turn the glass right way up.

7

● Move your left hand under the glass and, as you do so, bring the perspex disc below the glass again, where it will stick of its own accord.
● Now simply pour the water into the bowl. No one will see the perspex disc under the glass and the method you have used in the trick will remain a real mystery.
● Put the glass into the bowl of water, wipe your hands on the towel, and get on with the next trick.

✖ HANG ABOUT

Another opportunity to defy gravity – this time using empty beakers.

Effect

The performer shows a handkerchief to the audience, places the handkerchief on a book, positions two tumblers on the handkerchief, and then proceeds to turn the book and the tumblers upside down. The tumblers are suspended in the air, apparently defying gravity!

Equipment

A large, coloured linen handkerchief. Two 5 mm (⅕ in) diameter coloured beads and thread matched to

the colour of the handkerchief. A sewing needle. Two
lightweight plastic tumblers. A medium-sized hardback
book.

Preparation
Sew the two beads onto the handkerchief about 5 cm
(2 in) from the mid-fold (**1**). The distance between the
two beads should be about 3 mm (¼ in) more than the
width of your thumb.

1

Place the handkerchief on a table with the book and the
glasses and you are ready to perform.

Performing
● Hold the handkerchief up to show the audience, but
keep the side with the sewn-on beads towards you so
they cannot be seen.
● Fold the handkerchief in half with the beads on the
inner surface of the upper half (**2**).
● Lay the handkerchief on the book and tuck three sides
of the handkerchief under the cover of the book to stop
the hankie hanging down later in the trick (**3**).

2

3

● Now hold the book, with the handkerchief on top, in your right hand with fingers underneath and thumb on top. The thumb must be carefully positioned between the two beads (**4**).

4

● Pick up one of the tumblers and place it upside down on top of the handkerchief; this is apparently a casual move, but in reality you wedge the tumbler's rim between one bead and your thumb (**5**).

● Now place the second tumbler, also upside down, alongside the first, with its rim wedged between your thumb and the other bead. Both tumblers are now trapped securely between your thumb and the beads.

● Now turn your hand over (**6**). The tumblers do not fall to the ground but remain apparently suspended underneath the book – much to the amazement of the audience.

5

6

- Wave your left hand above and below the book to show that there are no hidden supports – magic alone is responsible for holding the tumblers in place.
- As the audience applauds, turn the book over and remove the tumblers. Pull off the handkerchief and place it in your pocket. Turn the book spine uppermost and shake the book as if to see whether the secret will come tumbling out from between the pages. Shrug your shoulders and take a bow.

◆ TEN POUNDS TO A PENNY

An economical trick which uses very few props and depends on crafty presentation for its success.

Effect

The performer challenges a spectator to a friendly bet. Having lulled the spectator into a false sense of security, the performer turns the tables.

✚ Equipment

A book of paper matches. Pencil and paper. An electronic calculator.

Preparation

No special preparation is needed.

Performing

- Tear a match out of the book of paper matches and challenge a member of the audience to a friendly contest. Claim that when you flick the match in the air you can control the flight of the match and make it land on the side of your choosing. Saying this, mark one side of the match with a pencil line (**1**, see over).
- Get ready to flick the match into the air, adding as explanation to your challenger, 'When the match is in the air call out "marked" or "unmarked" and I'll make

1

sure the match lands with its other side face up. We'll
try the best of three.'
● Carry out the three tosses of the match.
Note: Which side is up when the match lands is largely
a matter of chance, and in all probability you will win
only one or two out of the three tries. Occasionally, you
will win none out of the three, in which case you are
well set up for the scam which follows. In a few cases,
you will have won all three tosses, in which case, you
can finish the trick there and then by saying, 'You try
it.' Repeat the three tosses of the match, but with the
other person tossing the match and you calling the side.
The probability is small that he or she can repeat what
you did.
● In most cases, you will have lost one or more times
and the challenger is now set up for the last part of the
trick. Continue with, 'Look, this worked OK the other
day. I'll tell you what, I'll bet you £10 that I make the
match land on its edge. In fact, I'll make it easier. You
bet a penny. If I win, you can pay me back over three
weeks – a penny on the first day, two pence on the
second, four pence on the third, and so on, doubling
each day, up to 21 days. If you win, I'll give you £10
straight off.'
● Having drawn the spectator into the challenge, just
before you flick the match, bend it into a C-shape
around your thumb (**2**).
● Flick the match into the air, and it is almost certain to

2

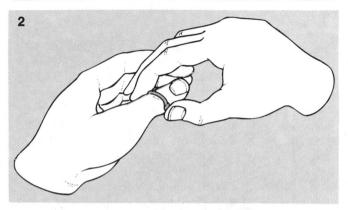

land on its edge. When it lands, add, 'Well, I didn't say what condition the match would be in when it landed!'

● When the spectator and the audience roar in disapproval, finally back down and say, 'Alright, I'll give way on the bet. It's just as well. I'll show you what you owed me.'

● With this, write out the four columns on the piece of paper and, using the calculator to help you add up, show just how much you would have won (**3**, see over).

● Finish with, 'I could have retired early on that!'

3

Day	Payout each day (in pence)	Total payout (in pennies)	Total payout (in pounds)
1	1	1	0.01
2	2	3	0.03
3	4	7	0.07
4	8	15	0.15
5	16	31	0.31
6	32	63	0.63
7	64	127	1.27
8	128	255	2.55
9	256	511	5.11
10	512	1023	10.23
11	1024	2047	20.47
12	2048	4095	40.95
13	4096	8191	81.91
14	8192	16383	163.83
15	16384	32767	327.67
16	32768	65535	655.35
17	65536	131071	1310.71
18	131072	262143	2621.43
19	262144	524287	5242.87
20	524288	1048575	10485.75
21	1048576	2097151	20971.51

GRAND TOTAL = £20,971.51

✖ THE RING IS THE KEY

An astounding trick. This one will have your audience
truly perplexed.

Effect

The magician makes a borrowed ring disappear from a
wine glass. The ring is found attached to a clip inside a
key case. The case has been in the audience's view
throughout the trick.

Equipment

A wine glass. A thick linen handkerchief, a needle and
colour-matched thread, and a metal ring about 15 mm
(½ in) in diameter. A key case of the fold-over press-
stud type containing a row of clips (**1**). A jacket with
top pocket and side pockets.

1

Preparation

Bend one of the key clips open so that a finger ring will
easily slip onto it (**2**, see over). Then attach three or
four keys onto the remaining clips.

2

Close the key case so that the open clip hangs outside the case (**3**) and place the case in your left pocket. Prepare the handkerchief by knotting the metal ring onto the thread and then attaching the thread to the centre of the handkerchief so that the ring, when hanging down, does not extend beyond the edge of the

3

handkerchief (**4**). Place the handkerchief in a top pocket with the ring well concealed.

4

Performing
● Borrow a finger ring from a spectator and hold it in your left hand. With your right hand, take out your handkerchief and in full view of the audience place the ring under the handkerchief (**5**).

5

● As you do this, secretly palm the spectator's ring in your left hand (see p. 32).
● Bring the threaded ring up under the handkerchief (**6**).

6

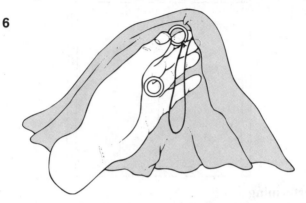

● Hold the threaded ring in your right hand through the material and give this to a second spectator to hold (**7**).

7

● Put your left hand (containing the palmed ring) into your left pocket and quickly attach the ring to the open clip.
● Bring the case out of your pocket, making sure you conceal the clip and ring behind your hand (**8**).

8

● Ask the spectator with the hankie to hold it over the glass and then to release the ring so that it drops into the glass (**9**).

9

● With your right hand reach across and whisk the handkerchief away and put it back in your top pocket (taking with it the threaded ring).

● Ask the first spectator to retrieve her ring from the glass. When she tries she will discover that the ring is no longer there.

● At this point, open the key case, and turn it to face the audience so that the keys are hanging down. There in the middle of the row of keys is a ring attached to a clip (**10**).

10

● Unhook the ring from the clip and hand it to the first spectator. She will verify it is hers. This should meet with appreciative applause – your audience will be genuinely baffled.

✖ CUPS AND BALLS

A variation on the oldest known conjuring trick. This trick can be performed as a mime, i.e. in silence.

Effect

Using three beakers and three small paper balls, the magician makes a ball appear to pass through a stack of plastic beakers. This illusion is repeated once, and then once again. At the end, as if revealing the secret of the trick, the magician shows that he was using a fourth ball all along. When revealed, this fourth ball is much larger than the others and could not possibly have been used to perform the trick.

Equipment

Three opaque plastic beakers that nest (fit together). Four 5 x 5 cm (2 x 2 in) squares and a 25 x 25 cm (10 x 10 in) square of the same coloured tissue paper. Table covered with a cloth. A jacket with side pockets.

Preparation

Roll the squares of tissue paper into four small balls and one large one. Place the large ball in your left pocket. Put one small ball in each cup and nest the cups together as shown (**1**, see over). Conceal the fourth small ball in your left hand using the palm technique (see p. 32).

Performing

● At the start of the trick pick up the three cups and hold them horizontally, with the fourth small paper ball still concealed in your hand (**2**).

● Now slide off the top cup and in one smooth movement place the cup in position on the table cloth.

Done quickly and smoothly, the paper ball will remain
inside the cup (**3**).

1

2

3

● Repeat this movement for the other two cups so that the three cups and their concealed balls are in position on the table (**4**).

● Tap each cup and lift the first to reveal a ball beneath it. Lift the cup with your right hand and casually place it into your left, its mouth over the concealed ball, as you direct the audience's attention to the ball on the table.

4

The second and third cups are lifted to reveal two more balls. As you pick up these cups nest them on top of the one in your left hand (**5**).

5

● Now place the three cups mouth down behind each of the balls. The first two cups are placed to the right and left positions and the third cup (containing the concealed ball) is placed in the centre (**6**). The audience is unaware of the fourth ball.

6

● Pick up the centre ball from the table and place it on top of the centre cup, and then nest the other two cups on top (**7**).

7

● Tap the top cup and lift all three cups as one to reveal a ball on the table. It appears that the ball has moved from the middle to the bottom cup (**8**).

8

● Once again place all three cups on the table but place the middle cup (containing the extra ball) in position over the centre ball on the table (**9**).

9

● Place the right-hand ball on top of this cup, then repeat your previous actions to make it apparently pass from the middle to the bottom cup – and reveal two balls on the table when you lift the three cups together.
● Repeat these actions once more but place the left-hand ball on top of the centre cup and then, when all three cups are nested, get a member of the audience to tap the top cup. While this is happening you have ample opportunity to steal the large ball from your pocket and hold it concealed within your left hand.
● Lift all three cups as one to show that there are now three balls on the table. Casually place the nested cups into your left hand and over the concealed large ball (**10**).

10

● Put all three cups on the table, with the large ball concealed beneath the bottom cup. The fourth ball remains hidden between the bottom and middle cup. This action should be done casually as if you have finished the trick.

● As if an afterthought, as you place the cups on the table pick up the three balls one at a time and say, 'Sometimes people accuse me of using more than three balls when I do this trick. Who thinks this is the case?' Look around the audience and when you have found someone who thinks so, add, 'You're right. In fact, I use four. This is the extra one.' As you say this, lift all three cups as one to reveal the large ball on the table and take your bow.

● Dispose of the beakers carefully so that no one finds the hidden fourth small ball.

◆ THE INDESTRUCTIBLE BALLOON

A baffling balloon trick, suitable for all age groups.

Effect

The performer inflates a long balloon, inserts it into a tube, and then proceeds to push several knitting needles through the tube and into the balloon. The needles are removed, and the tube then handed to a spectator. He takes out the balloon which, amazingly, is still intact.

✚ Equipment

Several long, strong balloons. A cardboard or plastic tube about 7.5 cm (3 in) in diameter and about 12.5 cm (5 in) in length. A skewer or similar hole-punching device. Spray paint. Five smooth, slim, steel knitting needles.

Preparation

Take the tube and, with a skewer or similar device, punch ten holes around its middle (**1**) – five holes on one side of the tube and five holes on the other. The position of the holes is important. They should be staggered in two rows so that five knitting needles can be pushed through from one hole to another, leaving a central region inside the tube through which no needles pass (**2**).

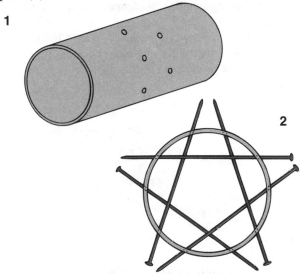

1

2

Once constructed, the tube can be decorated using spray paint. Check that the tube has no sharp edges which could puncture the balloon – any such defects must be removed.

Start the trick with the tube, the knitting needles and a selection of balloons on a table in full view of the audience.

Performing

● Ask a member of the audience to choose freely one balloon out of the several provided.

● Now show the tube to the audience and explain and show that there are several small holes around the centre line of the tube.

● Hand the knitting needles to someone in the audience to inspect.

● Now take the chosen balloon, lower it into the tube, and start to inflate the balloon. Keep checking the balloon, so that it protrudes equally from either end of the tube (**3**).

3

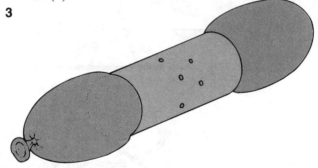

● Make sure you do not inflate the balloon too hard, but just enough for the balloon to be gripped securely by the tube. When you are satisfied, knot the neck of the balloon.

● The trick depends on you being able to twist the inflated balloon secretly so that a waist is introduced which effectively divides the balloon into two (**4**). Do this by distracting the audience momentarily, perhaps by asking for the return of the knitting needles. As you drop your hands to take back the needles, secretly twist one end of the balloon two complete turns away from you (**5**).

4

5

● Now take a needle in your right hand and hold up the tube in your left hand but with your thumb secretly inserted between the tube and the balloon (**6**, see over). The thumb allows you to check that the waist of the balloon is in the correct position, aligned with the holes. It also enables you to check that you are guiding the needles correctly from one hole to another and around the balloon.

● Now, carefully insert a needle from the back (your

side) through one hole so that it exits through a hole at the front (the audience's side). Use your thumb to guide the needle. When inserting or removing a needle, do so slowly. Friction will cause the balloon to burst if the needle is rubbed harshly along its side. Now hold up the tube so that the audience can see the tube from all sides and see that the needle does pass right through.

● Continue in this way, inserting one needle at a time, until all five needles are in position (**7**). Hold up the balloon and take a bow.

6   **7**

● Now, slowly and carefully, remove the needles one at a time, again with your thumb in position.
● Just before removing the last needle, secretly untwist the balloon so that the waist is removed.
● Now hand the balloon to a member of the audience and get him to slowly remove the last needle.

● Take the intact balloon out of the tube and hand the
balloon, tube and needles to the audience for them to
inspect. Take a well-deserved bow.

◆ SAYING GOODBYE
A magical way of saying goodbye at the end of your
performance.

Effect
The performer folds a plain banner in half, inserts a
length of red ribbon and then unfolds the banner. The
word 'Goodbye' is now magically revealed, written in
red ribbon.

Equipment
Three pieces of soft, dark material, all the same colour
and size, about 40 x 30 cm (16 x 12 in). Two pieces of
red ribbon about 1 m (3 ft) long. At least 5 m (15 ft) of
colour-matched sewing thread, a sewing needle and
chalk. A metric ruler. Glue (optional).

Preparation
Place one piece of material on the table and lay a
second piece on top of it. Sew the two pieces together
along the top edge and exactly halfway down each side.
Open out the two unsewn flaps and place these flaps
against the third piece of material. Sew this third piece
onto the other two pieces so that you now have a three-
sided banner as shown (**1**, see over).
Across one side write, in chalk, 'Goodbye'. Then sew
or glue one of the red ribbons over the chalk to form the
word (**2**).

Performing
● Pick up the banner and hold it with the written side
folded down as shown (**3**).

1

2

3

● Raise both bottom edges to the top, so forming two pockets (**4**). Into the rear pocket place the length of red ribbon.

● Now change hands, and as you do so, release your grip on the outer fold (the one facing the audience). The flap falls, revealing the message 'Goodbye' (**5**).

● Take a bow and leave the stage, hopefully to well-deserved applause.

4

5